LET HER HEAR

LET HER HEAR

Parables from a Mom

Sonya Contreras

🐂 Bull Head Press

Published by Bull Head Press
Squaw Valley, California
Paperback ISBN:978-0-9907237-4-5
eBook ISBN: 978-0-9907237-6-9

Library of Congress Control Number 2016918927

Cover Design by Wendy_graphics at Fiverr
Formatting by Joseph Contreras, Jr.
Typeface: Felix Titling, Bell MT, and Constantia

Printed in the United States of America.

"He who has ears to hear, let him hear." Mark 4:9, 23

Dear Reader,

It is a common trend to read devotionals: a quick five-minute glance at the Scriptures so we can hang onto something throughout our day.

We do well to look to the Scriptures for that glimpse, but God wants more from us. He wants our hearts all day, not just for five minutes.

These parables do not substitute careful study of the Word. They give a starting point to focus on where God wants you to be all day, a help to see Him even while doing the mundane, routine, necessary, "mom" things in life. They remind us of the heavenly realm that's part of the earthly walk.

Parable literally means "cast alongside" something else.

Jesus's parables were stories cast alongside an earthly event to illustrate a truth. He united earthly things with heavenly meanings to illustrate truth.

When the Jewish leaders rejected Him, Jesus turned exclusively to parables. When His disciples asked why, He responded, "He who has ears to hear, let him hear" (Mark 4:9, 23).

Jesus told parables for those who sought God's truth.

Some only heard the story.

But others, seeking God's truth, had ears that heard.

My parables, too, may be read by many as just stories. But to those moms struggling to find that glimpse of the heavenly realm through their hectic, demanding, earthly lives, "let her hear" truths of what one mom has heard from her Savior.

Sonya Contreras

These parables have been taken from articles previously written for my website and made into book form.

TABLE OF CONTENTS

GOD'S GIFT

C hrist came as God-man to die. Why?
    For us.

Why must someone die for us? Because we could never satisfy a holy God's requirement of perfection. We sinned. (All of us.) We fall short of what God wants, so He sent His Son to die, a substitute for us, so that God's holiness could be satisfied.

He died for all of us, but that doesn't automatically make us acceptable in His presence. We must accept His Work in our lives: allow Christ's blood to cleanse away our wrong. His requirements will then be satisfied.

All who have never accepted Jesus's gift remain sinners, doomed for judgment until they take God's offering of Christ's death for their sins, and acknowledge Him as Lord and Savior of their life.

Fancy prayers are not what He wants. Simply tell Him you've sinned. You fall short of His holiness. But recognize His Son paid for all sins on the cross when He died. Ask for His blood to clean you from all your sin. Thank Him.

It's a gift. It's a gift more precious than any other anyone could ever receive, but it must be accepted for it to be yours.

Knowing about Jesus is not knowing Him. Do not be like the demons who know about Jesus and tremble. Know Him and be His.

WHY CARE?

Why do you get up in the morning? Do you love your job? Do you thrive with the challenges of the day?

I can sympathize with a friend who once told me, "I get up to let my dogs out. That's it."

The boys had finished with school, the sun was calling us to go outside. We got our gloves (we have stinging nettle all through our garden) and went to the garden. One look told me we could be there until nightfall and still not make a dent in the weeds. Why bother? We all put in an hour of weeding (that's all I could do), and called it a day.

But the thought kept growing in my mind, Why care? I certainly didn't, or I would have been more disciplined and stayed longer to make the garden look better.

Sometimes I look at my house with the same attitude. Why bother? It's a mess. I'll just shut the door and not use that closet. I'll go to another room and not see the dirty dishes. I'll just...How far can I go before the mess catches me and hits me in the face?

Why care? The answer must be better than to get up for my kids and my husband...because sometimes getting up to listen to one more page of c-a-t, cat, d-o-g, dog is not enough.

I recently read the book *Story Craft* by John R. Erickson (better known as the author of Hank, the Cow Dog).

He states that authors have a responsibility to write books of beauty because we are made in the image of God and we are to reflect His beauty.

As the saying goes, "God doesn't make junk."

Guess that means we shouldn't be satisfied with ugly, either.

Or my messy house.

Or my weedy garden.

In the daily routine of growing children, my house was commonly messy.

I understand the Proverb "without the oxen the manger is empty." When you use big animals, you're going to have big messes to clean, but by using them, you do more work.

Or when I do remodeling or painting, the mess is bigger before it gets better. That's to be expected.

Now as my little children have somehow gotten bigger than me, I must re-evaluate what is essential for my time and efforts. The boys clean the house. We are down to only two at home during the day. It's amazing how the dirt level has gone down (exponentially). So I don't enforce cleaning some things every day anymore. But that makes it easier to get sloppy in enforcing any "clean." (Is that why babies of the family tend to be less disciplined? Their mothers have lost all their energy!)

But one hour of weeding with only three people is not as effective as with five people. We still make progress, but I find myself wondering, do we need this big garden?

Why care?

Some days I feel like I just slop together a meal. It's gone in 15 minutes anyway. So does it matter?

My motivation goes back to what Erickson said, being made in God's image and reflecting His beauty. Isn't that why we notice the beauty of a flower? Or the ugliness of ... my closet?

We, as moms, are made to make our homes reflect our God—His order, beauty, and cleanness. We reflect Him.

I'm inspired when I shop with my sister at stores she likes. They reflect calmness, creativity, peace. I like to go to her house where she has tastefully decorated things. It's like going to an expensive hotel, only feeling at home.

Why care?

Because you can create that feeling of peace, calmness, and beauty in your home, too.

It must first start inside, where the attitude says, "I do care, because God made me to be like Him."

That attitude influences what you do in your corner, your closet, your house, your yard.

You can find the beauty because God has put it there.

You have to let go of the clutter, of what you think is important, and see Him.

Why care?

Because God cares.

ARE YOU GOD'S?

If God has called you to be really like Jesus He will draw you into
a life of crucifixion and humility, and put upon you such demands of obedience, that you will not be able to follow other people, or measure yourself by other Christians, and in many ways He
will seem to let other people do things that He will not let you do.

Other Christians and ministers who seem very religious and useful may push themselves, pull wires, and work schemes to carry
out their plans, but you cannot do it, and if you attempt it, you
will meet with such failure and rebuke from the Lord as to make
you sorely penitent.

Others may boast of themselves, of their work, of their suc-
cesses, of their writing, but the Holy Spirit will not allow you to
do any such thing, and if you begin it, He will lead you into some
deep mortification that will make you despise yourself and all your
good works.

Others may be allowed to succeed in making money, or may
have a legacy left to them, but it is likely God will keep you poor,
because He wants you to have something far better that gold,
namely, a helpless dependency upon Him, that He may have the
privilege of supplying your needs day by day out of an unseen
treasury.

The Lord may let others be honored and put forward, and keep
you hidden in obscurity because He wants to produce some choice
fragrant fruit for His coming glory which can only be produced in
the shade. He may let others be great, but keep you small. He may
let others do a work for Him and get the credit for it, but He will
make you work and toil on without knowing how much you are
doing; and then to make your work still more precious, He may
let others get credit for the work which you have done, and thus
make your reward ten times greater when Jesus comes.

The Holy Spirit will put a strict watch over you with a jealous love and will rebuke you for little words and feelings or for wasting time, which other Christians never feel distressed over. So make up your mind that God is an infinite Sovereign and has a right to do as He pleases with His own. This may not explain to you a thousand things, which puzzle your reason in His dealings with you but if you absolutely sell yourself to be His love slave, He will wrap you up in a jealous love and bestow upon you many blessings, which come only to those who are in the inner circle.

Settle it forever, then, that you are to deal directly with the Holy Spirit and that He is to have the privilege of tying your tongue, or chaining your hand, or closing your eyes in ways that He does not seem to use with others. Now, when you are so possessed with the living God that you are, in your secret heart, pleased and delighted over this peculiar, personal, private, jealous guardianship and management of the Holy Spirit over your life, you will have found the vestibule of heaven.

Anonymous

ALONE

I Kings 18:1-19:18

Ever feel alone?
I find, especially when I am in the heat of a trial, I do. I think
I'm the only person who has this problem.

Beware of the Enemy's tactics to isolate, divide and conquer, and
breed defeat.

When I was a young mother with baby and toddlers, I knew of
others whose husbands stayed home two weeks from work after
their child was born. Mine didn't. He went to school or work the
day after the birth. The Enemy planted seeds of isolation in my
mind, in spite of my mother-in-law's help.

I read books telling of women settling the West. They gave birth
and managed the farm while their husband hunted for their sur-
vival. Then I did not feel so alone. Others had lived to journal
about it. I found strength through their victory.

Sometimes the Enemy wishes me to wallow in that aloneness
when my husband must be gone for long days, for long nights, for
a year of deployment several times.

Whenever that "aloneness" creeps over me, I remembered the
Enemy wishes to divide and conquer our relationship. My husband and I minister together. I create a haven at home for him to
anchor his heart. He tells the world about Christ. He can leave
because I support him. I can support him because I know his heart
is here with me. The ministry continues. The Enemy is defeated.

At times, I'm tempted to tell him, "Stay home. Don't go. Quit the
Army." But just as quickly, I realize his ministry gives him purpose.
The home would no longer be a haven for his heart to rest; it
would confine his spirit in a cage. I swallow my words, because I
know what compels my husband, what motivates him, what

drives him. And I also know God gives me the grace to do my ministry—make our house a home.

If he were to stay at home when he should be involved in the ministry God has given him, he would be like David when he stayed from warring with his men. He would be idle. Something else would fill his time—something not God-given.

Look at Elijah. The land of Israel had no rain. The famine came. Elijah told King Ahab to prepare an altar and call to Baal for his blessing.

After waiting an entire day, watching the priests shout, slash themselves with spears, and beg for Baal to listen, Elijah repaired the altar of the Lord. He poured twelve barrels of water over the altar, its wood, and the bull. Water filled the trench surrounding the altar.

Then Elijah prayed.

Fire of the Lord consumed the sacrifice, the wood, the stones, the soil and the water in the trench.

The people worshiped, "The Lord is indeed God."

Elijah commanded the priests of Baal to be slaughtered.

King Ahab quickly demanded, "Where's the rain?" (Victory doesn't last long.)

Elijah, with confidence in his God, commanded the king, "Eat and drink, for rain is heard."

Then Elijah climbed to the top of Mount Carmel and put his face between his knees.

His servant looked toward the sea six times reporting to Elijah, "There is nothing." The seventh time, he said, "A cloud as small as a man's hand is rising from the sea."

Elijah warned King Ahab to hurry to his palace before the rains came.

Elijah was doing God's Work, God's Way. He had just experienced a miracle—two—the fire accepting the sacrifice and the rain sent by God.

Now, Queen Jezebel wasn't happy with Elijah killing her Baal-worshipping priests. She issued a death-warrant for Elijah.

Elijah ran.

Elijah succumbed to say, "Take my life; I'm no better than my ancestors." Then he slept.

Beware of aloneness when you're tired, weary and burdened.

I'd get angry at my toddler's refusal to sleep after rocking him so long. I wanted to scream at him. Within minutes after wanting to scream, he'd be asleep. Couldn't I wait just 5 more minutes?

When you're tired, you feel alone—sleep. Motherhood is a hard, physical job when the children are young. I never could get enough sleep. I never slept through an entire night from when I was pregnant with our firstborn till our seventh finally could sleep through the night at age three. (That's about 18 years!) Tiredness opens the door for feeling alone.

Notice what happened after Elijah slept, an angel touched him and said, "Get up and eat." He did.

Many times we are just too tired and too weak to think properly. God gave his prophet sleep. He gives His own sleep. "Come to me, all you who are weary and burdened, and I will give you rest. Take my yoke upon you and learn from me, for I am gentle and humble in heart, and you will find rest for your souls. For my yoke is easy and my burden is light" (Matthew 11:28-30).

Aloneness comes when we are tired, weak and perhaps doing things God doesn't want us to do. His yoke is easy. If the task is too heavy or too burdened, maybe the task isn't for you to do. If you are feeling God left you to carry too much, maybe you should see if the task is something God even wants you to touch. That "aloneness" is not from the Enemy but from your Friend Who carries the burden He gives you, not the burden you put on yourself. Give Him your burden and don't take it back.

Let's look again at Elijah's complaints to God when God asked him, "What are you doing here, Elijah?" Why was he hiding in a cave, sleeping?

Elijah replied, "I have been zealous for the Lord. The Israelites rejected You, broke Your altars, killed your prophets. I am the only one left, and now they are trying to kill me."

(Did the Lord acknowledge Elijah's aloneness? Did He sympathize with his feelings?)

Then the Lord said, "Stand on the mountain in My presence." (Can you be alone, in God's presence?)

Elijah stood in the opening of the cave.

A great wind tore the mountain apart and shattered rocks before Elijah's presence, but the Lord wasn't in the wind.

A great earthquake split the ground under Elijah. But the Lord wasn't in the earthquake.

A fire consumed all that lived around Elijah. But the Lord wasn't in the fire.

Was Elijah ready to acknowledge God?

When Elijah heard the gentle whisper of the Lord, he pulled his cloak over his face.

"What are you doing here, Elijah?"

Elijah had his response memorized; he had convinced himself of its truth. "I have been zealous for You. The Israelites have rejected You, broken Your altars, put Your prophets to death. I am the only one left and now they are trying to kill me, too." (Sounds like a repeat of before, doesn't it? He hadn't stopped feeling sorry for himself.)

Elijah's aloneness consumed him so that he couldn't even acknowledge he was in God's presence. He was still standing, speaking to the Lord Almighty. He hadn't fallen on his face before God. He thought his burden, his job was so important God couldn't do without him. He didn't realize he had forgotten his dependence upon God for His ministry.

His aloneness was self-imposed. He wasn't looking to God to carry his burdens. His job was right, but he was carrying it alone.

The Lord told him, "Go back to anoint Hazael king over Aram. Anoint Jehu over Israel. Anoint Elisha to succeed you as prophet.

Yet... Yet I reserve 7,000 in Israel—all whose knees have not bowed to Baal."

Elijah had 7000 people believing as he did. He had others to continue what he had started. He was not alone. He felt alone because he carried his burden. It was the right burden, but he didn't allow God to carry it for him. God took it away and gave it to another—Elisha.

Beware when God's burden becomes your burden. If you carry it without dependence upon Him, the burden will be too heavy.

Aloneness can be the Enemy's way of bringing discouragement, your body's way of telling you to rest, your Friend's way of prodding you to give the burden to Him. Check when you feel alone. His promise remains true since the day He said it, "I am with you always, to the very end of the age" (Matthew 28:20).

ARE YOU STRESSED?

A re the little things overwhelming you?
The little ones are sick, you can't sleep, your days are just holding babies and wiping noses ... wondering if this flu will ever be over. You can't keep your eyes open, even to change a diaper.

I've also been in such a big hurry, doing so many things, that I didn't know who I was and what I should be doing. It wasn't just physical tiredness, I was tired to the bone, emotionally.

That's when the verses of Matthew bring comfort and perspective.

"Come to Me, all who are weary and heavy-laden, and I will give you rest. Take My yoke upon you and learn from Me, for I am gentle and humble in heart, and You will find rest for your souls. For My yoke is easy and My burden is light" (Matthew 11:28-30).

Can you imagine Jesus in a hurry?

He told his disciples he must go to Jerusalem...but he didn't rush to get there.

What important things do you have to do today? Things that didn't get done yesterday must be done today.

Wouldn't God have more pressing things to do, than you?

Yet he was never in such a hurry that he "lost" his kindness, his gentleness, his peace.

If you are burdened, are you doing something God didn't want you to do?

Do you need to say no to good activities in order to do the best? "My yoke is easy..."

Having a yoke is still work, but it is easy.

Are you taking more than you should? Are you doing your job and your husbands? Are you trying to make the decisions for your grown children?

"My burden is light."

God didn't make you a mom so you can rule the world, or your family.

He made you a mom so you could learn from Him.

Are you stressed? Go to Him and He will give you rest.

BEING IN JESUS'S PRESENCE

"The clearest view I ever got of the ugliness of my sins was not in reading the Ten Commandments but in being near to Jesus in that awful darkness on the cross" (Smith, p. 72).

How close are you to Jesus?

When Isaiah saw God, he said, "I am undone. I am a man of unclean lips."

His words, his works, his heart didn't come close to what God wanted for him.

He didn't find excuses.

He didn't justify his actions.

He stood before God in truth.

He could do nothing.

It is easy to judge others.

Why don't they do this?

Why can't they choose right?

But when we get closer to Jesus, He lets us see ourselves.

How close do you let Jesus come to you?

Do you keep Him at a distance so He won't see what you do?

So you don't have to change?

So you can do what you want?

Or do you allow Him to see all the hidden places of your life,

the fears no one else knowns,

the insecurities that keep you from trusting Him,

the areas you must control because you know better?

To be close to Jesus means to allow His light to shine on your darkness.

Light reveals.

Penetrates.

Exposes.

Changes.
Once the light reveals what you are doing, you can't continue to sin.
You can't enjoy it without becoming hard.
I like things to be the same.
I like a good cup of tea.
I want my day to carry on, like yesterday.
No surprises.
No hassles, problems, inconveniences.
But those things make me go to Jesus.
He pushes me toward Himself.
I see more of my unsubmissive attitudes,
my independence,
my desire for what I want.
He shows me my wrong.
He takes away the dross.
He forgives the sin.
He changes me.
I become like Him.
What's your response after being with Jesus?
What does spending time with Jesus do for you?
Do you come away with joy? Bless Him? Worship?
"And they worshiped Him ... with great joy. And were continually in the Temple blessing God" (Luke 24:52-53).
Source:
Smith, C. S. (2015). *Heaven, How I Got There: The Story of the Thief on the Cross*. Scotland, UK: Christian Focus Publications.

HARD TIMES

Perhaps we all feel like there is too much "need" for the money in our pockets.

Consider these prices:

One gallon of gasoline ------------------------- $0.16
One quart of oil ------------------------------- $0.15
Haircut -- $0.25
Roll of toilet paper --------------------------- $0.25
Telephone bill --------------------------------- $2.25/month
Three pounds of rice --------------------------- $0.18
One gallon of milk ----------------------------- $0.12
One dozen eggs --------------------------------- $0.22
A bakery-type apple pie ------------------------ $0.10
Two loaves of bread ---------------------------- $0.10
Two pounds of butter --------------------------- $0.25

Do you envy the good old days?

Consider those prices with life during those times. It was 1930, the Great Depression. The average income from 1930-1933 was $3 a week, if you could work. Many couldn't find jobs ... and they actually *tried* to find work.

We had a vacuum cleaner that didn't work (for my children's sake, this was not during the Great Depression). We scraped the rug with a brush to take off the cat and dog hair stuck to it. I remember thinking, "If only we had a vacuum cleaner that worked." What ecstasy when my husband brought home a vacuum cleaner—brand-new and heavy-duty. Within a month, that new vacuum couldn't suck up the dirt. Do we have that much dirt?

I have slowly learned new doesn't mean better and improved doesn't mean perfect. Although I know it in my head, working it out in daily life has been an exercise in re-learning. My motto, "We are not in heaven yet" reminds me life is not perfect. "This world is not my home, I'm just a passin' through." I will have perfect in heaven—not here.

When I remember these things, I can evaluate a purchase better. Do I really need another _____? Will it really solve all my problems? I don't purchase as many things, and I am happier with less (junk).

I complain (in my mind) less. I understand things aren't going to last forever (Do I really want this rug to last forever? (Then I couldn't get a new and improved one!)

I choose to be content.

Paul was not a woman who likes to spend money, but he did have a verse for me. "I have learned to be content in whatever circumstances I am. I know how to get along with humble means, and I also know how to live in prosperity; in any and every circumstance I have learned the secret of being filled and going hungry, both of having abundance and suffering need" (Philippians 4:11-12).

When I think of contentment, an illustration from C.S. Lewis comes to mind. He described a distinguished lady who just wanted "a cup of tea." She complained when no one could make her that perfect cup of tea. The demon, who was instructing another, explained if she was consumed with that cup of tea, she was not a threat to their mission. Am I not a threat to pursuing God's mission, because I just want a perfect cup of tea?

How much is God's mission jeopardized because I can't be content?

Hebrews 13:5 "...being content with what you have."

Paul wasn't debating on a new convenient tool or product.

When did he write these words?

Paul may have received a scrap of food and dirty water which he shared with rats. He sat on a cold, stone floor but couldn't lean against the wall because of the wounds on his back. He didn't have a septic system, other than the end of his chain. Light didn't reach his cell, so darkness was all he knew. His companion, if he had one, was unkempt and smelled as bad as he.

But he was content.

"Godliness with contentment is great gain" (I Timothy 6:6).

Guess I don't need that carpet.

Guess I should be content.

Makes me look forward to heaven where perfect actually exists, and where the rug won't even be missed.

CONTENTMENT —IT'S NOT FOR THE TIMID

Ever wonder why God is teaching you the same thing, over and over again? Maybe you're a slow learner and aren't getting it? I think, "I've learned this already. Can we move on?" It's the same lesson again—only deeper.

So in case you're saying I've written about this before (I have because I learned it before), you are getting it again (because apparently God thinks that I need a refresher course).

Contentment comes on the heels of thankfulness. Someone once asked, "What if God only gave you today what you thanked Him for yesterday?"

My list of thankful options has broadened with that in mind, but apparently, my depth of thankfulness needed to be tested again.

We were having water pressure issues. We always do. We can't water the front yard and the back yard at the same time. We have low pressure inside if we water outside. But in July the inside faucets were just trickling with nothing else running.

Our pump was sounded. The water level was not covering the pump. The serviceman said, "Conserve and allow the water to seep back before using it."

For those of you back East, we do not get rain in the summer from April until November. No Rain. The option of water 'seeping in' to fill all our needs until November was not a pleasant, thanksgiving moment.

We cut back laundry from 3-5 loads a day to 1 sometimes 2 a day. (Don't look too closely at the boys' clothes. They will be dirty.)

We did not use the dishwasher—but had select boys who can clean dishes. (Otherwise I wash them, so I can eat from a clean spoon—another thing to be thankful for.)

We brought water to fill our water tank—for animal and garden needs. (We watered the garden every three days now, and only one section. When the fruit trees look almost dead, we water those, too.) Our lawn, that the boys worked so hard to make green is dead. My roses are dead. I won't continue my list, for then I will have trouble being content.

The boys refrain from flushing bathroom facilities. (I cringe, for I know what training is required to make sure they're not peeing off my back porch.)

All these things we do, and I thank God I can still turn on the faucet and have running water. But the one thing I have difficulty being content without is showers.

I problem solve in the shower.

I relax. When I wake up and cannot move without pain, I soak up the heat from a good long shower.

I escape without interruption (the boys have to be bleeding and dying to call me in the shower.)

My husband has informed us how to take a military shower. Turn on water and get wet (do not wait for proper temperature) TURN OFF. Suds up. Rinse off. Get out.

Nice thought. Here's the problems:

I do not like COLD water. I do not like soap drying on me before rinsing.

I get tangles in my hair that don't come out unless I comb them under running water with conditioner.

I can't solve other problems when I'm trying to hurry and save water.

I definitely cannot relax in COLD water.

This is not an escape for stress—this IS the stress. How many gallons of water go down the drain with one shower? Will the pump last until the rains comes? When will it rain?

You can believe I thank God better for the water I now have.

And pray that we will continue to have running water. (Notice I'm getting more specific with my thanks.) Hauling water from outside to flush toilets is not what I want for my weight lifting program.

[I won't even tell you about my two phones not working for the past two months. I could only receive texts, not calls, from one. The other phone wouldn't even ring when we got a call. If we did have a dial tone (sometimes), we'd be cut off within minutes. So I couldn't even call my phone company to complain... Did I tell you God was working on me about contentment? And thankfulness?]

First Timothy 6:6 says, "But godliness actually is a means of great gain when accompanied by contentment."

Is contentment the key to gaining godliness?

My measure of godliness while under the COLD water is not very high. God continues to show me the blackness of myself, reminding me that I need to get closer to Him to see the light, feel the warmth, and know the cleanness of being washed by His Word.

Contentment. It's not for the timid. It's not for stubborn. It's not for my own comfort.

Contentment. It's for Him. Because He deserves my thanks.

MEDITATIONS FROM EXODUS 19–20

If you were to meet God on a mountain top, what would you do to prepare yourself?

(19:10, 11) God told Moses to prepare the people, yet they were staying at the bottom of the hill. They were to consecrate themselves for two days, washing themselves and their garments. They were to be ready on the third day.

How do you make yourself ready to meet with God? How do you hear the voice of the Lord?

The Lord told them to consecrate themselves. Prepare. Focus.

What does consecrate mean? J.I. Rodale's *The Synonym Finder* gives these descriptive words for consecrate: sanctify, hallow, make holy, bless, anoint, canonize, beautify, deify, devote, dedicate, pledge, promise, vow, commit, consign, assign, apply, give, honor, esteem, revere, bow down to, glorify, extol, exalt, praise, laud, celebrate, magnify.

Notice all the verbs—action verbs implying doing something, and not just with your body but with your mind, your heart, your being. You engage everything. You focus.

(19:12, 13) How did God help them to focus? He commanded a boundary to be put on the mount to keep the people away. Is there a place where you can limit interruptions? Where the cares of this world do not push into your mind to hinder what God is saying? As a mom, especially of young ones, you wonder if you will ever go to the bathroom by yourself!

One mom would throw her apron over her head to pray. Her ten children knew she was praying. Find a big apron, snatch a moment—maybe after a midnight feeding, to consecrate yourself before the Lord.

Do you have a chair you can stick in a closet so you cannot see the messy house, or the laundry that needs to be folded? Can you stand by the window and look out, without seeing the dirt on the window, to focus? He is waiting before He comes to the mount. The boundaries are set.

(19:20) The Lord descended on the mount and He called to Moses. That gives me great comfort. He knows me by name. He calls me. John 10:3 says, "He calls his own sheep by name." (And that name is not Mom.) He knows my dreams and my heart-aches.

(19:21-23) When Moses reached the top, the Lord sent him back to the people. "Go back and remind the people to stay back." As a mom with needy little ones, God doesn't expect us to forget the little people while we talk with Him. He calls us to protect them. That helps me not feel guilty that I grab only a moment with the Lord nor get angry when I am interrupted by those I serve.

(19:24) But then Moses returned to the top. He stood with Aaron. Sometimes we enter God's presence with the help of others. We stand united and we hear His voice. Aaron and Moses heard the commands. They returned and shared with the people what God spoke.

(20:18-26) Moses returned alone to the mount. Aaron stayed behind. Sometimes, He calls us to come alone before Him. What does He tell us? What we need to hear. Hard words. "I am a jealous God. Put nothing between Me and you."

He gives boundaries for the people who have been without direction for four hundred years. God gives a way to serve. "Make a tabernacle to worship."

So I leave Moses on the mountain receiving the words from the Lord. He was gone forty days. The people grew restless. The people forgot Him. The people looked to other things, even while the mountain smoked, rumbled, and quaked.

Do I wonder how my boys can forget my commands so soon? They are not focused on my words, but on their wants. Am I any different?

We have made ready to meet with God. We are consecrated.

We have separated ourselves from others. We are alone.

We have been called.

What now?

We listen. (Another action verb requiring work, putting away my wants to hear His.) But that is for another time, for we have made ready.

ARE YOU LISTENING?

Sometimes we misunderstand each other. I heard something that wasn't said. I felt an attitude that wasn't meant.

Recently I texted my son asking how work was going. (He was helping at church with the two younger boys.) He responded, "Great."

Later when he made a comment about how bad it was with one of the boys, I asked, "But you said it was 'great.'"

He gave me that look of incredulous disbelief. "Mom...it didn't have an exclamation point."

"And...? What does that mean?" I ignorantly asked.

"It was sarcasm. It couldn't get any worse."

I laughed. So without a punctuation mark, one word indicates the end of the world? (I better edit my writing better!) "I'm sorry. When I received "great,", I stopped worrying about whether the boys were listening, and helping. Instead, I should have been praying harder.

My husband and I were talking. (Yes, we do that.) He said something. So I acted upon it. Later, he said, "I thought I told you to wait."

I considered. "I thought you decided to do it, but just had to process how you would complete the task."

That wasn't what he meant ... I have to remind myself that I'm like Paul—get rid of John Mark, he's a hindrance. And my husband is like Barnabas—let's help a brother out, let's consider, let's wait. (I hate waiting, by the way.) I somehow heard only part of it. My husband is patient with my "leap ahead and do it" attitude, I'm not so patient with his "wait and see." But we sometimes make communication work. Maybe, I think...

Sometimes I wonder if I even listen to people. How could I get it so wrong? Am I like that with everyone, all the time? If I can't even hear people, how do I hear God?

God brings me to these times to slow me down ... think on what He is telling me ... listen with my heart.
If I can't hear God, then I'm not listening.
If I'm not listening, then I'm too busy.
If I'm too busy, then my tasks are my idols.
Ouch.
Puts things in perspective, doesn't it?
"Be still and know that I am God" (Psalm 46:10).

BECOME LIKE A CHILD

Have you ever been around a child?
They're excited with life. They are thrilled with little things.
There's not a dull moment with them. They live life with enthusiasm. It's like a constant party.

Do you hear how they think? I grow weary of the silliness from my son...I try not to listen. I get discouraged. When is he going to grow up? When will he think about consequences? But then I really listen to him. "Mom, my fish doesn't like soggy food."

"What makes you think that?"

"He won't eat it if it falls apart in his water."

"How do you think you should feed it?"

"I don't know."

"Think about it, and let me know what you should do."

"Mom, I want to walk in the moonlight so I can find all the shiny rocks."

"How will you find them without the sun shining on them?"

"In the moon, they will glow in the dark; the sun hinders me from seeing them."

"Mom ...."

His connections aren't quite right and common sense doesn't reach him...but then God reminds me, "God has hidden these things from the wise and intelligent and has revealed them to infants. Yes, Father, for this way was well-pleasing in Your sight." (Matthew 11:25)

God shares His delights with children.

They hear His Words. They are delighted.

Why?

They treat life like a gift, like a package to be opened moment by moment. They don't doubt, but trust. They live the wonderment of wanting to know. Look at this...Why does this happen? What makes this go? They believe without proof. They trust simply.

Have you lost that child-like faith?

I have lived long enough to know the fairy world doesn't happen, that people aren't to be trusted, that miracles happened in the Bible, but maybe not now...Losing that child-like innocence, that child-like wonder, that child-like view makes believing harder, trusting more a chore, life more routine. Common sense hinders me from trying something different that might work better. Knowing what could happen makes me hesitate to even try.

Matthew gives hope, he said, "become like children." We can go back. "Truly, I say to you, unless you are converted and become like children, you will not enter the kingdom of heaven. Whoever then humbles himself as this child, he is the greatest in the kingdom of heaven. And whoever receives one such child in My name receives Me; but whoever causes one of these little ones who believe in Me to stumble, it would be better for him to have a heavy millstone hung around his neck, and to be drowned in the depth of the sea." (Matthew 18:5-6).

Many times, I've made decisions that went against common sense. I didn't have money, but God was prompting me to go to grad school anyway...I obeyed. God provided. I learned to trust like a child, to believe He would provide. I delighted Him. A step toward becoming like a child...

Children don't think about what could happen...they think about what they can do. They are free to fail. They aren't hindered. They can fly.

What is the Spirit prompting you to do, but your common sense is telling you, "It won't work?" Become like a child. Put away your fears, doubts, even your common sense that keeps you standing on the platform. Become like a child. Spread your wings.

Fly.

And delight God.

WHAT YOUR REACTIONS
SAY ABOUT YOU

How do you respond to your family after a bad day?
Reactions are not pre-meditated, planned, or logical.
They're emotional responses, showing what's inside, who you really are.

Circumstances do not control your reactions.

Growing up the saying "the devil made me do it" was popular. It eliminated my responsibility. I could do what I wanted and blame the devil. Today, we are "more educated," instead we blame our parents and our upbringing for how we are.

But are we responsible?

Why disciple our children, if what they did, was not their fault?

What does the Bible say?

Proverbs 23:7 says, "For as he thinks within himself, so he is."

"A good man out of the good treasure of his heart brings forth what is good; and the evil man out of the evil treasure brings forth what is evil; for his mouth speaks from that which fills his heart." Luke 6:45.

What treasures you store in your heart determines whether you are good or evil. (I'm not talking saved or not, we all are sinners. "There is none good, no not one.")

So, I am responsible. Even when words fly out of my mouth faster than I can catch them? Yes!

How do I stop hurtful words?

Some people try to stop them at their lips. They try more will-power and self-control.

Does it work? No. The Bible even says that it won't. "His mouth speaks from that which fills his heart."

I don't stop the hurtful words at my lips, but at my heart.

I must change how I think.

How?

By "taking every thought captive to the obedience of Christ..." II

Corinthians 10:5.

"Have this attitude in yourselves which was also in Christ Jesus...." Philippians 2:5.

"Do not be conformed to this world, but be transformed by the renewing of your mind ..." Romans 12:2

We change how we think. We do not dwell on how we were mistreated, or undeserving of wrong. We fill our hearts with what is "true, honorable, right, pure, lovely, of good repute, if there is any excellence and if anything worthy of praise, dwell on these things." Philippians 4:8 paraphrased.

What fills your heart?

Have you heard the expression, 'dirty old man'? Did he just happen to become that? Or was that what he thought about all his life, but now he isn't hindered by what people think?

What is filling your heart today? It is preparing you for hardship. How will you respond?

Let me apply this further...

Do you enjoy your husband?

Or do you wish that he was someone different?

Are you angry with your husband? He's late again. Why won't he help you? Why doesn't he discipline the children the way you do? Why doesn't he help with the children more?

You are becoming a whiny woman...with no good in her heart. You are discontent with your husband. That is how you will respond when he is late from work, when he doesn't do something like you would do. You will respond with what you've filled your mind.

Do you want a happy marriage?

Then you must change the thoughts you think about your husband.

You cannot berate him in your mind, and serve him with your hands. They work together. Jesus would say, "You hypocrite!"

Change your thoughts, so you can help him.

Are you his helpmeet?

"For as she thinks within herself, so she is."

Who are you, really? Time will tell.

ARE YOU IN A RUT?

Routine: daily, treadmill, habit, rut, beaten path, regular, ordinary, usual.

If you sleep eight hours a night, you will have slept 219,000 hours by the time you are 75 years old (not including any naps).

If you brush your teeth twice a day for two minutes each time, for seventy-five years, you will have spent 109,500 minutes or 1,825 hours brushing your teeth in your lifetime.

Routine builds your day, and your life.

Yet when you return from a vacation, do you remember how many times you brushed your teeth while you were gone?

Of course not, the routine slips from your mind, and the exciting adventures stand out.

As the Israelites traveled across the desert, the routine was their life. Water was essential. Food became important.

They arrived at the Promised Land, ready to enter in a year and a half. That's one and a half years of eating and drinking water!

But then they have no faith. They're not ready for the land. They wander for forty more years. Forty years of the same routine!

In their routine, they found water and food were gifts they must ask from God.

Exciting? No.

Adventurous? No. Just routine.

The daily life of God's people who were beginning to know their God.

Yet God planned to bring them to see Him.

If God felt routine was what they needed to know Him, how are we any different?

Look to see God in your routine.

Jesus told his disciples, "He that is faithful in the little things, shall inherit the earth."

How much of that inheritance will you have, when the little things are considered?

HABITS THAT BIND

Habits are automatic responses that require no conscious thought.

Habits are good. They schedule our day.

We drive without consciously thinking about putting our foot on the gas, steering, and braking. When our sons started driving, no one was allowed to talk. The student-driver concentrated on what he was doing. (So did I.) The other boys remember how quiet our trips to town were. We celebrated when he could take a drink of water while he drove. (And I allowed him.) Then it became a habit, an automatic response. He didn't have to think about braking. It became a response.

Our day is full of habits. We wake up, when? We do the same thing today as we did yesterday. The day becomes a habit. Those habits are what children need. Structure. Boundaries. Guidelines. When the children are in school, they do morning chores first, breakfast next, and school starts by 8 AM.

If every day was a guess, I'd spend my day answering questions and stabilizing their insecurities. With habits, they know what to expect and what to do next.

Even dinner becomes a schedule: spaghetti on Wednesdays, pizza on Friday, Mexican on Saturday. Allows energy for important things, like discipline or doing things the boys enjoy.

But what about those habits that aren't good? Those attitudes that tell you, "You can't do it, you're no good, you might as well not try." What about those excuses, "I'm too tired to discipline my child this once"? What about dessert, just this once, when I'm on my diet?

When do those concessions become a habit? When you give in, give in and give in again. We know when we are doing it—at first. Later we don't even think about it.

"Take captive every thought to make it obedient to Christ." II

Corinthians 10:4 Every thought. That's how we don't allow bad habits to start.

Researchers tell us that it takes thirty days to start or eliminate a habit

What if we have 'given in' and now it's a habit? Instead of automatic pilot we must think about the action every time and consciously choose to do right. Several things can help.

Change your schedule. Although schedules are good, they set you for 'automatic pilot.' People quitting smoking automatically want to light up after eating dinner. Change your ritual to avoid the temptation.

The habit is a process—breaking the habit will also be a process. It takes time (at least thirty days.)

Find a buddy. "Though one may be overpowered, two can defend themselves. A cord of three strands is not quickly broken." (Ecclesiastes 4:12)

Remember, you are not alone. You cannot make yourself more holy. It's not trying harder, being better, doing good. You can't. You need God reminding you each time. His Spirit reminds gently. You need God to help resist. Pause. Listen. Obey.

Replacement principle. Take away and replace. Do not leave a vacuum.

Ever notice when someone tries to quit smoking they often gain weight? They've replaced smoking with eating. Be careful what replaces the wrong. (I'm not picking on smokers, but it is a habit that we can all visualize.)

"When an evil spirit comes out of a man ... (he) returns to the house he left. When he arrives, he finds the house swept clean and put in order. Then he ... takes seven other spirits more wicked than himself, and they go in and live there. And the final condition of that man is worse than the first." (Luke 11:24-26)

"Hate what is evil; cling to what is good." (Romans 12:9) Find the weakness of the habit and develop the strength. Are you a complainer? Learn thankfulness. Are you discouraged? Show faith. For every negative trait, there is a positive one. Cling to the good.

Consequences. Often the habit's consequences are not seen for a long time.

A person who smokes the first cigarette doesn't picture himself carrying around his oxygen in order to breathe. "It won't happen to me" attitude keeps the knowledge of the consequences away.

Realize the long time effects.

Yet, knowledge does not change behavior. (Look at all the heart surgeons that smoke.)

Many times bad habits are really sin. Recognize it, confess and forsake it. (Pepsi is not evil. But if it controls how I feel, then I've allowed it to master me—I only need one Master and that is God. I must allow God to control my feelings. And so, I limit Pepsi. Deep sigh.)

With sin, we often obey because we fear the consequences, not because we desire to please God. We accept salvation because of the assurance of heaven not because of God's presence. Fear of consequences shouldn't drive us; pleasing God should.

Guard your heart. "Above all else, guard your heart, for it is the wellspring of life." (Proverbs 4:23).

What you think about, you become. Do I want to be a nervous, complaining person?

Dwell on what is good. No! Dwell on Who is good—for I cannot be "good" on my own.

"Let your eyes look straight ahead, fix your gaze directly before you." (Proverbs 4:25)

Attitudes reflect your focus. Overconfidence shows pride. Doubt gives way to fear. When I'm easily bothered by "things," I must re-align my focus.

Peter walked to Christ on the water. When he looked to his circumstances, he faltered. Christ was the one Who held Peter up—Peter just gazed on Christ.

"Let us fix our eyes on Jesus, the Author and Perfecter of our faith, Who for the joy set before Him endured the cross, scorning its shame and sat down at the right hand of the throne of God. Consider Him who endured such opposition from sinful men, so that you will not grow weary and lose heart. In your struggle against sin, you have not yet resisted to the point of shedding your blood." Hebrews 12:2-3

Habits—they help and they bind. Which ones did the Lord press on your heart today? How's your focus?

HAVE STRESS? READ A BOOK

"Come to Me, all who are weary and heavy –laden, and I will give you rest. Take My yoke upon you and learn from Me, for I am gentle and humble in heart, and you will find rest for your souls. For My yoke is easy and My burden is light." (Matthew 11:28-30)

My husband reminds people who are stressed that if they are doing what they should, they won't be stressed. The answer isn't less work or less hours or a vacation; it is doing His Work. Christ's burden is light. He even puts on His yoke—a tool for plowing and working, yet He gives rest. The work isn't the stress. When the work becomes the stress, then evaluate the work. What is His work for you?

The question lies not in how can I find more time in the day to do everything? But what should I be doing? And what should I not be doing? His burden is light. Much of our stress is self-induced by trying to do things He doesn't want us to do. What should you let go? The result: You will find rest for your soul.

Many times, it is not the work that causes the stress, but the emotional trauma with the work. The accounts kept, numbers balanced, bills paid, children disobey. Life happens.

I've learned not to ask my boys, "Why did you do that?" They give me that blank look. They have no idea. They did it without thinking. They have no idea "Why?" Now I'm angry I asked them and they can't answer. So for my sanity, I don't ask "why." A simple way of reducing emotional stress. My burden is light.

During those emotional trauma times, the part of the verse that says "Come unto Me" becomes significant. When I come to Him, I receive perspective; I focus; I have rest.

Why is this article titled "Got Stress? Read a Book"? Part of that "come unto Me" implies knowing His Word, reading it, learning it, living it. The easy part is the reading. The next step requires a conscious effort. The living it demands the Work of the Spirit. But then I have rest.

The University of Sussex in 2009 researched the benefits of reading on heart rate and muscle tension. They concluded that even six minutes of reading can be enough to reduce stress levels by 68%. Compare this to

Listening to music   61%

Drinking a cup of tea or coffee 54%

Taking a walk 42%

Playing video games (brought heart rates 21% down from highest level,

but left heart rate above starting point)

Dr. Lewis, who conducted the test, said, "Losing yourself in a book is the ultimate relaxation...It is more than distraction but active engaging of imagination as words on printed page stimulate your creativity and cause you to enter what is essentially an altered state of consciousness."

Do we do that when we come to Christ's Words? Do we enter to absorb the words? Or do we read with our mind somewhere else? Do we find rest in His words because His Spirit is allowed to flow through the words to calm our spirits and still our hearts so we can have rest?

Yes, reading reduces stress. But coming unto Him eliminates it. Does that mean we won't have stress? Of course not. Are we perfect? I'm not. But we know where to go when we have stress. He gives rest, not only for the body but for the soul.

Sources

The Telegraph. "Reading 'Can Help Reduce Stress'." The Telegraph. March 30, 2009.

http://www.telegraph.co.uk/news/health/news/5070874/Reading-can-help-reduce-stress.html (accessed March 2014).

HE OPENED THEIR MINDS TO UNDERSTAND THE SCRIPTURES.

Luke 24:45

Has your mind been opened?
We get stuck in ruts.
We think the same way.
We do the same things.
Routines are good.
Einstein had four identical suits so he wouldn't have to waste time thinking about what he would wear for the day. He could concentrate on what was important to him.
Habits form from thought patterns.
People wake up and must have coffee, (Me, I have Pepsi.)
Now I must have coffee to start my day.
We see things from one side. (What's wrong with coffee?)
We begin to believe that is the only way. (What's wrong with you, if you don't drink coffee.)
We also approach the Scriptures with certain expectations.
We only see what we want to see.
Jesus must open our minds to understand His Scriptures.
To see Him, not as we expect, but as we should.
What has Jesus showed you from His Word that was different from what you believed?
Has Jesus opened your mind to really understand the Scriptures?

WHAT DOES IT TAKE TO KNOW GOD'S HEART?

His Words convey His attributes. He told man His Words. His Actions portray His Values. His Actions puts feelings behind His Words. They authenticate His message. He loved the man He created.

His Heartbeat can be felt when one listens to His Words and looks to His Actions.

God sent His Son, to meet us where we were, sinful, unloving, needy.

What motivates God?

He longs for our love returned.

He gave His truth.

He showed His Justice.

He proved His Love.

His Words and Actions show His Heart.

His heartbeat stopped when His Son died to give us life. Through His Son's death, He enabled us to come to Him. He helped us love Him.

When we just follow His rules, we don't feel His heartbeat. We only seek to obey enough not to experience His Judgement. Obedience brings us closer to Him, but not to His passion.

God wants a relationship with us. He wants us to know Him.

If God is motivated to know us, what should we be motivated to do?

Do we know Him?

HOW SECURE ARE YOU?

Colossians 1:13-20

Ever think about gravity? Gravity keeps us planted on the ground.

The sun's gravity keeps the earth in place, otherwise the earth would fly in a straight line rather than in an elliptical path around the sun.

What is gravity?

We define gravity by what it does. It keeps our planets and galaxy in orbit with the universe. Gravity keeps our sun in orbit. Gravity keeps earth traveling around the sun. Gravity keeps the moon orbiting our planet. Gravity keeps us here on earth.

But what is it? Scientists don't know.

The answer is found in Colossians 1:17 "He (Christ) is before all things, and in Him all things hold together."

We are held to our planet by Christ. We are held to our solar system by Christ.

What about the atom? The atom's center containing protons and neutrons.

What charge do protons have? Positive.

What happens when 'like' charges come together? (Think magnet.) They repel.

So why doesn't the nucleus of every atom fly apart instead of stay together? Again, scientists don't know.

I find the answer in Colossians 1:17 "in Him all things hold together."

Every atom's nucleus is held together by Christ.

Protons in the nucleus have a positive charge. Electrons fly around the nucleus in orbits with a negative charge. What keeps the electrons from falling into the nucleus due to the positive pull of the protons? (Think magnets—opposites attract.) Scientists tell us that virtual photon give an electromagnetic force that keeps the electrons from collapsing into the nucleus. What are those virtual photons? Light made of electromagnetic waves.

Again, scientists define it by what it does. They describe virtual photons in the quantum theory.

How does the atom stay intact without collapsing into the nucleus? God told us, "In Him all things hold together."

Ever think about when Christ comes back. All those dead bodies turned to dirt must form bodies again. How? Just like at creation when man was formed from dust. What gives all those elements life? We can explain the electron bonding of the elements, and the carbon structure of its proteins, but how did it come together and be alive?

God told us, "in Him all things hold together." Colossians 1:17

Man lives as if God is not here. We blame our weather on what we do. We think we control our own destiny.

I find comfort in knowing God is present in our every-day life, in our every-day moments. In fact, without Him, all things would not be held together. The Creator God controls it all—nothing catches Him by surprise, nothing is outside of His power. After all He holds even the atoms together, He holds me to this earth and to this galaxy. He gives me life.

That gives me peace. I can trust Him.

He is God.

Is it any wonder that the next verse in Colossians says, "... so that He Himself will come to have first place in everything."

He is supreme. He is God.

Why does He do this?

"It was the Father's good pleasure for all the fullness to dwell in Him and through Him to reconcile all things to Himself, having made peace through the blood of His cross; through Him, I say, whether things on earth or things in heaven." Colossians 1:19-20

Gravity, atom structure, creation—what does that have to do with you?

We are held together by His power. We are made for His good pleasure not only by His creative acts but by His redeeming works. When Christ spoke of those who knew His Father, He promised, "No one can snatch them out of My Father's Hand." John 10:25-30

Since God holds all things together, I can trust Him to hold me, redeemed by His Son, in His Hand through eternity.

"What then shall we say to these things? If God is for us, who is against us? ... Who will separate us from the love of Christ? ... (Nothing) will be able to separate us from the love of God, which is in Christ Jesus our Lord." Romans 8:31-39

If God holds me in His Hand, then He keeps me there. I don't worry about my temporary life. I have no concern about my eternal home. He secures my destination. Why should I worry?

> *O Love that will not let me go,*
> *I rest my weary soul in Thee.*
> *I give Thee back the life I owe,*
> *That in Thine ocean depths its flow*
> *   may richer, fuller be.*
>
> *O Light that follow'st all my way,*
> *I yield my flick'ring torch to Thee.*
> *My heart restores its borrowed ray,*
> *That in Thy sunshine's blaze its day*
> *   may brighter, fairer be.*
>
> *O Joy that seekest me through pain,*
> *I cannot close my heart to Thee.*
> *I trace the rainbow through the rain,*
> *And feel the promise is not vain that*
> *   morn shall tearless be.*
>
> *O Cross that liftest up my head,*
> *I dare not ask to fly from Thee,*
> *I lay in dust life's glory dead,*
> *And from the ground there blossoms*
> *   red life that shall endless be.*
>
> *George Matheson, 1882*

Gravity, atom structure, life, eternity...All held in His hand. I have peace. Don't you?

HURTING PEOPLE

There's a lot of hurting people.

My son brings home students who ask to come to his house because they heard "It was peaceful." Their families fight or aren't even together. They want to go somewhere where they don't have to be someone. The hurt goes deep with no easy answers.

How do you help?

Some hurts are caused by sin.

Love is not the answer.

If loving a sinner could make them change, we wouldn't need prisons.

A mother's love would keep her son from jail.

Knowing consequences is not the answer.

If simply knowing consequences would cause right choices, we'd have no sinners.

The leading heart surgeon in our area built a hospital and a heart center around him. He died of heart disease caused by smoking. Knowing not to smoke didn't change his actions.

We all have a choice. As the Bible says, "All, we like sheep, have gone astray."

People must reach bottom before they look up. No one else can make someone do right. They must want to change.

When given a choice, we sin.

Man left to his own devices is a miserable creature.

It takes God to choose right.

Mothers soften the consequences of wrong choices their children make. The father disciplines "too hard," so the mother undermines his authority and doesn't support his discipline. She helps her son out of the mess he's created by his wrong choices, before he even feels the sting of his wrong.

God gives consequences to make us change. We don't like change. We won't change unless we are forced. What motivation is there for change, when the mother softens the blows? Next time, God must hurt more to get her son's attention.

Remember the prodigal son? His father loved him enough to let him go.

Letting go, so God can correct our "out-of-the-home" children requires a greater love then trying to control the situation. Let go and allow God to work.

How can you help when he won't change?

That's when you pray.

God has given me discernment. I can see people heading for trouble, but I can't make them change. I can confront, which I do when His Spirit leads me. But most of the time, the Spirit shows me so I can pray.

We recently talked with the boys about their friends' influence. Bad company corrupts good morals. (I Cor 15:33) They didn't like it. They didn't want to see. They think I imagine things.

I feel the witch (again) for restricting and reminding.

Some people hurt, not because of their own sin, but because someone around them is choosing wrong.

Give them to God and leave it in His Hands.

God will do right.

"The Lord is near.

"Be anxious for nothing, but in everything by prayer and supplication with thanksgiving let your requests be made known to God.

"And the peace of God, which surpasses all comprehension, will guard your hearts and minds in Christ Jesus." Philippians 4:5-7

He guards my heart and gives me peace. The Lord is near.

DON'T GROW WEARY.
DO GOOD.

November is the month that we enjoy the harvest of what we have grown the entire year. We prepare for the Thanksgiving meal from the bounty given. It's a time of reflection of what the year has brought. With it comes recognition of God's faithfulness through another year. This is the month that I review all our family's activities and events to find what key thing we have learned from God. Every year God amazes me with how He brought us through each event.

My son reminded me that we should thank God for the people in our lives. Usually I am wishing that I could live in a cabin in a wood away from everybody. (People can be annoying.)

Who in my life has encouraged me this year?

As I think, my list grows longer and so do the memories.

People are the blessing that help us through life.

It's that little note that encouraged me on the day when everything went bad. It's that smile in my son's face when I just yelled about something. It's that 'thank you' for the meal when I had thrown it together. People. My list grows...it's those people who influence my boys to do big things, man things. People. It's those who drop everything and help so we can have water. People. It's even those people who annoy me, because they are also the ones who bring me flowers and say, "See the rock I found, Mom." It's the People.

I can say like Paul, "I thank my God in all my remembrance of you, always offering prayer with joy in my every prayer for you all..."

Paul doesn't just thank these people who have made a difference in his life. He blesses them. The next verse he tells them, "For I am confident of this very thing, that He who began a good work in you will perfect it until the day of Christ Jesus" Philippians 1:3-6.

Christ's works would be made perfect. What He has started in their lives will not be in vain.

What kind of blessing can I share with those who've helped me?

My hands are empty for I cannot repay the gentle words, the smile, the skill, the perfect timing... but I am reminded of Paul's words again.

"Do not be deceived, God is not mocked, for whatever a man sows, this he will also reap... Let us not lose heart in doing good, for in due time we will reap if we do not grow weary. So then, while we have opportunity, let us do good to all people, and especially to those who are of the household of the faith." Galatians 6:7-10

Do not lose heart in doing good. Do not grow weary. Do good.

God will perfect your works that He has started. As you do, may "the grace of our Lord Jesus Christ be with your spirit, brethren. Amen" Galatians 6:18.

ROBERT MURRAY MCCHEYNE: A LIFE NOT WASTED

Much of this chapter will be quotes from his diary. He inspires, encourages, and exemplifies a life sold to Christ alone.

He only lived 29 years, and in his brief seven and a half years of ministry, he did more that will last for eternity than many have done in a lifetime.

After David, his elder brother, died, Robert wrote, "I lost my loved and loving brother, and began to seek a Brother who cannot die." He felt the worthlessness of his own endeavors to please God. Not only did David's death bring his own salvation, but impressed eternity's nearness upon him. He prepared for the ministry to 're-deem the time.'

Preparation (1831-1835)

At college, he was influenced by men like Chalmers and Welsh. He read biographies of past ministers, especially Jonathan Edwards, Brainerd, Martyn, Payson and Halyburton.

McCheyne adopted Edwards Resolutions:

1. Resolved never to lose one moment of time, but to improve it in the most profitable way.

2. Resolved, that I will live so, as I shall wish I had done when I had come to die.

3. Resolved, to live with all my might, while I do live.

From a letter to another student, he wrote: "Do get on with your studies. Do everything in earnest. Above all, keep much in the presence of God. Never see the face of man till you have seen His face who is our life, our all."

The last entry of his student days in March 29, 1835: "Life is vanishing fast, make haste for eternity."

His Ministry (1835-1836)

In his message, "If the Gospel pleased carnal men it would not be the Gospel. The Spirit's first work in salvation is to convict of sin and to bring men to despair for their condition by nature. A broken heart alone can receive a crucified Christ."

Urgency and alarm characterized his messages.

"The only power that can bring a child of Satan and make him a child of God is God Himself."

His aim was to bring his people to see the "vastness, completeness, and freeness of the salvation brought by Christ...it is only the truth of God which the Spirit will honor and bless."

Though always conscious that souls were perishing every day, he never thought a minister's main work consisted of outward activity. "The great fault I find with this generation is, they cry that ministers should be more in public. They think that it is an easy thing to interpret the word of God and to preach."

His heart was in the work, his hand was not slack.

He said, "'Lord, what will Thou have me to do?' It was answered, 'I will show him how great things he must suffer for my name's sake.' Thus it may be with me. I have been too anxious to do great things. The lust of praise has ever been my besetting sin; and what more befitting school could be found for me than that of suffering alone, away from the eye and ear of man?"

And McCheyne did suffer.

July 8 "Lord, I will preach, run, visit, wrestle," said I. "No, thou shall lie in thou bed and suffer," said the Lord."

His ministry was a soul confiding in the faithfulness of God. Constant fellowship with God was the safeguard of his soul. Preaching the Gospel was his great delight.

The honor of Christ and the love of souls were the great rules by which he lived—his chart and compass amidst the storm.

His Christian Walk

"I have never risen a morning without thinking how I could bring more souls to Christ...every one of my flock must soon be in heaven or hell."

"Above all things, cultivate your own spirit. Your own soul is your first and greatest care. Seek advance of personal holiness."

"It is not great talents God blesses, so much as great likeness to Jesus."

"A word spoken by you when your conscience is clear, and your heart full of God's Spirit, is worth ten thousand words spoken in unbelief and sin."

He wished to be always in the presence of God.

"Some believers were a garden that had fruit trees, and so were useful; but we ought also to have spices, and so be attractive."

Bonar writes, "The real secret of his soul's prosperity lay in daily enlargement of his heart in fellowship with his God. Meditation and prayer were the very sinews of his work...He kept by his rule, 'that he must first see the face of God before he could undertake any duty.'"

His constant aim was to avoid any hurry which prevents 'the calm working of the Spirit on the heart. The dew comes down when all nature is at rest—when every leaf is still. A calm hour with God is worth a whole lifetime with man...'"

"It has always been my aim...to have no plans with regard to myself. That the place where the Savior sees meet to place me, must ever by the best place for me."

A fellow minister said, "His living presence was a rebuke...for I never knew one so instant in season and out of season, so impressed with the invisible realities and so faithful in reproving sin and witnessing for Christ."

He had such "continual dependence on Christ...have daily, hourly pardons. He ever lived as one on the brink of eternity, longed for a 'full conformity to God.' And prized communion with Him."

Mission to the Jews (1839)

During a time away from his church, when his health didn't permit preaching, he traveled to Israel.

"There is nothing like a calm look into the eternal world to teach us the emptiness of human praise, the sinfulness of self-seeking, the preciousness of Christ."

"God does not bless us in the midst of our labors, lest we say, my hand and my eloquence have done it. He removes us into silence, and then pours down a blessing so that all who see it cry out, 'It is the Lord.' May it really be so with my dear people."

"If you wish to gain a Jew, treat him as a brother."

"A foreign land draws us nearer to God. He is the only one whom we know here. All else is strange. Every step I take, and every new country I see, makes me feel more that there is nothing real, nothing true, but what is everlasting."

"We stood...where Jesus came and wept over it. And if we had had more of the mind that was in Jesus, we should have wept also."

Revival (1839)

While preaching in the open meadows at Dundee, heavy rain fell. The crowd stood till the last. The Word was listened with 'an awful and breathless stillness.' "Hardest hearts melted like wax before the flame; the most stubborn trembled, and bowed the knee to Jesus."

He declared, "Without holy fruit all evidences are vain...A real desire after complete holiness is the truest mark of being born again...Jesus first covers the soul with His white raiment, then makes the soul glorious within, restores the lost image of God, and fills the soul with pure, heavenly holiness. Unregenerate men among you cannot bear this."

Final Years

He warned his fellow ministers, "Our people will not thank us in eternity for speaking smooth things, and crying, 'peace, peace, when there is no peace.' They may praise us now, but they will curse our flattery in eternity."

"Every one of my flock must soon be in heaven or hell! ...I wished that I had a tongue like thunder, that I might make all hear; or a frame like iron, that I might visit every one and say, 'Escape for thy life. Ah, sinners, you little know how I fear that you will lay the blame of your damnation at my door.'"

Last diary entry January 6, 1843 "Often I would like to depart and be with Christ—to mount to Pisgah's top, and take a farewell look of the Church below—to leave my body, and be present with the Lord..."

He was anxious to leave no part of his work undone.

His last days were crowned with the beauty of holiness—it struck everyone who saw or heard him. Delirium overtook him on March 21. His utterances now showed the thoughts which were uppermost in his mind. "You must be awakened in time, or you will be awakened in everlasting torment, to your eternal con-fusion.' He prayed for his people, "This parish, Lord, this people, this whole place!"

He experienced severe suffering and frequent delirium until his death March 25, 1843.

His life showed his mission: "Oh, to be like Jesus, and with Him to all eternity." Over six thousand people attended his funeral. Robert Murray McCheyne (1813-1843) a friend of God.

Want your life to matter? Thirst for Him.

Sources:

Haslam, David. "The Robert Murray M'Cheyne Resource." M'Cheyne's Life and Times. 2010-present. http://www.mcheyne.info/life.php (accessed 2015).

"M'Cheyne and His Ministry: A Biography." Wholesome Words: Christian Biography Resources. n.d. http://www.wholesomewords.org/biography/bmcheyne8.html (accessed 2015).

SPEAKING TO HIM

We recently purchased plane tickets for a 'no-frills' ride. We could pick our seats for a charge. Consequently, most people were not sitting by their companions. The no frills came with cheapness.

The result was interesting.

At the beginning of the short flight, one woman talked loudly. I thought she was just a loud person...but as the flight progressed, I realized she was talking to her spouse five rows behind her. He was normally a loud person, but he chose to answer her with responses of patience, calmness and even enthusiasm.

She couldn't wait to tell him what she saw.

Their conversation wasn't of great importance...just what they saw out their windows, of what kind of city they were landing, their impressions of it. Her contribution was like a child—new and exciting; his response was like a teacher—telling about the city, growing fruits and vegetables for the world. She shared whatever popped into her head. "Look at all the houses!" He encouraged. "It's a city, all right." They didn't care who heard. They shared what they saw.

I saw through their eyes...It was my town. I already knew we grew fruit for the world. I hadn't thought my city was that much a city...I watched to see what they saw: the acres of food.

Is that what God hears when He listens to us? He enjoys the wonder we find in what He has made, even though it's not new to Him. He encourages us to share what He has done, regardless of who else hears. A steady conversation, sharing, telling what we see, so He can encourage, instruct, and perfect what He has started in us. Isn't that what He craves from us? To have communion with Him?

What keeps me from sharing with God? Is it the distance, not in rows, but in distractions? Have I stopped talking to Him because

I have found myself enough? He wants my thoughts to become like His. He wants me conformed to His likeness. How do I do that without talking to Him and hearing what He says? He's not looking for important words, or I'd fall short. He's looking for that child who says, "Look at that! I want to share that with You."

He wants us to know Him.

The flight may have been a no-frills flight, but the lesson learned was not cheap. It was worth a lifetimes of sharing, of telling, of listening.

My God wants to hear my words, regardless of how loud I shout and who else hears.

That's an incredible God!

WHAT DOES PRAYER DO?

Ever notice that moms worry? My sons tell me, "You imagine things that can never possibly happen." (Little do they know) I don't call it worry. It's my reminder to pray. When some uncertainty or uncontrolled event comes to mind, I tell the Lord.

When that same item comes to my mind again and again, I give it back to Him. That's petitioning Him. Like the widow who went before the king daily. He finally gave her request, not because he wanted to, but because he wanted her to leave him alone.

Sometimes, there's a gentle nudge...write that note, say that comment, call that person.

I excuse my disobedience. "I'm too busy." The nudging continues. I stop. I obey. I don't know why. That's intercessory prayer: praying for another who is struggling, who needs a kind word today, a reminder of life's worth, that cause to do what's right. Those prayers remind me I'm not alone. Others fight with me in the battle for right. God is on our side.

Sometimes what I want consumes me, weighs me down.

He waits to answer.

I demand, forgetting Who He is.

He reminds me.

I am humbled.

My need brings me to His feet.

That's where He wanted me.

I forget what brought me here.

He is enough.

God wants us to bring our needs to Him.

When I do, I find that the request is not the important thing.

He wants me to come.

He wants my fellowship. He wants my attention. He wants my concerns.

God doesn't need me. He wants me.

God wants to carry my burden.

So often I come with my hands so full I can't see over the piles.

He takes those piles from me, puts them out of my sight and says, "Now you've finally come, let's talk."

Why does it take the piles for me to come?

Why do those things even concern me?

I should just come.

Prayer...

Not because I get what I want. But because I am given what I need.

Not because 'things' work out. But because I look beyond the things to see Him.

Not because I no longer need. But because He is all I need.

Worried? Not anymore. God is near. He's all I need.

REST

Luke 10:38-42

How do you rest?
The picture of complete and total abandoning rest is when my babies slept.

Their schedule was off. They were crabby, fussy, crying. They would fight that rest.

Their 'unrest' would make me angry. Just sleep. That's what they needed.

But they would fight it.

When they finally closed their eyes and slept, quietness came.

And Rest.

Aren't we like that?

Sunday becomes a day to do on all that didn't get finished through the week.

Where's the rest?

We see Mary and Martha visiting with Jesus.

Martha is 'distracted' with the meal.

Food is pretty important. I get crabby if I don't eat.

Mary sits at Jesus's feet.

Who chose better?

Jesus said, "Only one thing is necessary, for Mary has chosen the good part."

Rest.

When you pray, but think of ten things you need to do, now.

Rest.

When your babies and little ones demand all your energy and you must leave the housework too.

Rest.

Jesus said, "Only one thing is necessary."

Where is your focus? What do you choose? Rest.

REMEMBER THE SABBATH, TO KEEP IT

W hy did God give this Command?
  "Six days you shall labor and do all your work. But the sev-
enth day is a Sabbath of the Lord your God...for in six days the
Lord made the heavens and the earth...and rested on the seventh
day; therefore the Lord blessed the Sabbath day and made it holy."
(Exodus 20:9-11)

Did God need to rest? Of course not.

But He knew the man He had made, needed rest.

Does any man admit he is tired, and needs to rest? (Of course
not. That would admit a weakness.) So God commanded man to
rest.

This command was not just for Israel as a nation. God's reason
came prior to Israel—at creation, when God made the heavens
and the earth.

When France lengthened her workweek to ten days without a
break, production decreased, accidents increased, focus dimin-
ished, sick days increased. When Russia made their workweek five
days, work didn't result in optimum production.

Do we question the Creator's time and design? He said, "Work
six; rest one."

How Did the Jews Remember the Sabbath?

Jews anticipated the Sabbath by cleaning, cooking, and preparing all day Friday. They had boundaries on what could and could
not be done on the Sabbath. They celebrated from sundown Friday to sundown on Saturday.

When Sabbath was over, they looked back to what they had
learned on the Sabbath.

It was the highlight of their week.

"Friday and Saturday come automatically, but Sabbath takes

place only when we make it happen. We prepare for 'Sabbath' by the clothes we wear, by the meals we eat, by the lighting of Sabbath candles, and by chanting the Kiddush over wine to set apart this special time."

How Should We Make the Day Holy?

God told Israel, "Keep it holy."

What does that mean?

Think of the normal day. We call it the work week, because we spend it on our needs. We need to eat, so we work.

But one day was God's.

He did not want it full of our 'stuff'.

He wanted our attention.

He wanted us to think on Him.

We sinned when we did not acknowledge Him in everything. The Sabbath helps us not to sin. It is a holy day.

When Should the Sabbath Be Celebrated?

Sabbath is on Saturday, the end of the week.

So why do we call Sunday, the "Lord's Day, the day of rest"?

The Jews celebrate the Sabbath. But the apostles designated the Lord's Day of rest at the beginning of the week. Some say this is because Christ rose from the dead on Sunday. It fit their calendar. The point was not what day, but they had 'a' day.

We are not 'under the Jewish law anymore' (Romans 6:14). We don't follow the Law. We have freedom in Christ, so "all things are lawful." (I Corinthians 6:12)

But consider the purpose of the commandment...

To remember.

To set aside.

To rest.

To make it holy.

Who Should Remember the Lord's Day?

Some of you may remember "blue laws"—state laws requiring shops and businesses to remain closed on Sunday. These laws reflected our "remembering our Creator."

Obeying laws do not make us holy.

Today, even the Little Leagues play on Sunday. Malls are crowded. It has become another day to do what we couldn't do yesterday.

Have we forgotten what God commanded at the beginning of time? Remember Him.

What Was the Jews' Punishment for Breaking the Sabbath?

A man picked up wood for his cook fire on the Sabbath.

Did God want him to starve? No, but He gave provision for His people to be ready for the Sabbath. He was without excuse.

His punishment: he was stoned.

How many stonings would happen today, if God enforced His day?

When the Jews entered their land, they were told to remember the Sabbath.

When they got busy and forgot, God made them rest. Another country conquered them. The land was given a rest. The people rested. And God was remembered.

What will it take for us, in our busy, hectic lives to see God and remember and rest?

The day is the Lord's. He wants us to spend it in worship, remembering, rest with Him.

Sources:

"Shabbat Customs." Reform Judaism.org: Jewish Life in Your Life. n.d. http://www.reformjudaism.org/shabbat-customs#sthash.wRWE-dea6.dpuf (accessed March 2016).

COMMITMENT

A re You Sitting on the Fence?
  Do you wait to see who is sitting on which side of the fence before you choose?

Do you go by what you feel like today?

Commitment is faith lived out. We get our faith from Christ by what we believe.

I believe marriage is 'until death parts us.'

I am committed to that decision, because God said it.

Because I start with that commitment, when my husband and I disagree, or I feel like running away, that isn't an option. We must work out our problems. My commitment helps me to obey God when it's hard.

God said that children are a blessing. My husband and I decided before we had any children, we would allow God to plan how many children and when we would have them. How many other blessings do you say, "No, I'm not ready now," or "We have enough"? When we gave that option to God, we didn't decide what form of birth control to use, God did. (We did breast feed on demand, weaning them when they were two years, so that spaced the babies out, but that is not a guarantee for some people.)

Did I want to reconsider that commitment after baby #___? Did I want to be sick more than half of my married life because I was hormonal and pregnant or recovering from giving birth? It wasn't an option.

When continuing to have children became a medical issue (I almost died after the last one), we prayed and decided to stop. But we believed God that children are a blessing. Eight sons later, we're glad we did.

We believe attending church is a vital part of a Christian's growth. Was it easy when we had five children under nine years and we lived an hour from church? Many weeks I spent walking the church hallway with a crabby baby, wondering why I bothered coming. He clearly led us to home-church for a time, but it was not an excuse not to attend regularly, it was obedience to His promptings. Now we again attend church with a group of believers. I sometimes wonder why God has brought us back, but I know He has. Our commitment to obey God keeps us going.

By making these commitments, our choices for other things were determined. By choosing to breast feed on demand, I had to be with the baby 24/7. That meant I stayed at home. That also meant that I couldn't attend every ladies' church function or serve much in the church.

That led us to living 'simply.' We homeschool. We have no television. Some things we searched out as Scriptures stirred our heart to change. Others we learned from godly couples who mentored us.

Our spiritual walk—is a walk. We learn. We listen. We grow. We change. Many of our choices went against what the world says. That made us different. We were criticized. People asked why? We are in the world but not of the world. We should be different.

If you are not different, if your commitments do not make you a people of God, are you listening to what He is telling you?

What do you believe? Do you search the Scriptures for your walk? If you found those answers, what are you doing about them? Once you chose to obey God, remember it will be tested, tried and given endurance.

"Why do you call Me, 'Lord, Lord,' and do not do what I say? Everyone who comes to Me and hears My words and acts on them, I will show you whom he is like: he is like a man building a house, who dug deep and laid a foundation on the rock; and when a flood occurred, the torrent burst against that house and could not shake it, because it had been well built.

"But the one who has heard and has not acted accordingly, is like a man who built a house on the ground without any foundation; and the torrent burst against it and immediately it collapsed, and the ruin of that house was great." (Luke 6:46-49)

What you believe, you will do. If you make your decisions based on what God says in His Word, you will not be shaken.

That fence board gets mighty hard sitting on it. And cold. As my son commented, "You don't sit there long." By choosing not to decide, you have disobeyed what God is telling you to do today. Where are you sitting? What do you believe?

ARE YOU WEARY?

Ever notice when you decide to do something 'right', you are immediately tested?

If I decide to lose weight, someone has a birthday and I have to make ice cream cake.

If I notice I should respect my husband more, he annoys me and I'm not nice.

If I tell myself I will not yell at my child, he requires more patience.

What about deeper things?

I know marriage is for life, but do I consider other options?

I know children are a blessing, but do I limit how many I have?

I know staying out of debt gives freedom, but what exceptions are acceptable?

Why must my commitment be tested?

Commitment is acting out your faith.

James 1:2 tells me, "Consider it all joy, my brethren, when you encounter various trials, knowing that the testing of your faith produces endurance."

Hebrews 11:1 defines faith. "Faith is the assurance of things hoped for, the conviction of things not seen."

Read through Hebrews 11. See the people who chose right, in spite of great suffering.

My faith is small—I'm not asked to sacrifice my sons. I'm not asked to die for my faith.

Hebrews 12:1-2 tells me to expect problems. "...let us also lay aside every encumbrance and the sin which so easily entangles us, and let us run with endurance the race that is set before us."

God tells me that I will get entangled by the 'stuff' of life.

But He also tells me how to win over it.

Where do I get this faith that stands against the testing?

Read Hebrews 12:2. "Fixing our eyes on Jesus, the author and perfecter of faith, who for the joy set before Him endured the cross, despising the shame, and has sat down at the right hand of the throne of God."

Christ was not just a good example of how we should be right and do good.

He is the source of our faith.

He is the perfecter of our faith.

Without Him, we have no faith.

What does that faith do?

Reread James 1:2. Faith gives endurance, "so that you will not grow weary and lose heart." (Hebrews 12:3)

Are you weary? Are you trying to stand for right and falling?

Are you doing it on your own?

You can't. Your faith will never be strong enough.

Focus on Him.

When I see Him, the ice cream does not tempt me.

When I see Him, the little annoyances don't bug me.

When I see Him, I can see others through His eyes.

Even with the bigger things, like having another child, when I see Him, I can choose to do what is right.

Or making the effort to resolve conflict with my husband, so that I can live with him.

Or believing God will provide without borrowing or living on credit, because He will provide my needs.

I see Him, and the things grow dim.

Helen Howarth said it well:

> *O soul, are you weary and troubled?*
> *No light in the darkness you see?*
> *There's light for a look at the Savior,*
> *And life more abundant and free.*
>
> *Turn your eyes upon Jesus,*
> *Look full in His wonderful face,*
> *And the things of earth will grow*
> *strangely dim*
> *In the light of His glory and grace.*

Is your faith being tested?

Look to him and don't be weary.

You will be given faith.

You will endure.

BEING IN THE WORLD BUT NOT OF IT: LOT'S STORY

Ever wonder about Lot, Abraham's nephew? He left his homeland with Abraham. He had chosen to follow Abraham in search of the land that God would give Abraham. Lot started out right.

When Abraham and Lot's shepherds fought over land, Abraham gave him a choice. Lot chose the good valley lands. He choose the best (Genesis 13:6-13).

His choice led him to move into the city (Genesis 14:11-12). What we choose today influences what choices we have tomorrow.

But then what? He became an important official in the city (Genesis 19:1, sitting in the gate refers to a leadership position).

When the city was taken captive in a battle, Abraham learned about it. He battled for his nephew. When Lot was rescued, he chose to return to the city.

Perhaps Lot used his position in the city for ministry. Was he influencing it for good?

What is the difference between living in the world and being a part of the world? When Jesus said, "If you were of the world, the world would love its own; but because you are not of the world, but I chose you out of the world, because of this, the world hates you." John 15:18-19

When God makes us His own, He does not remove us from this world. We're still here. But nor should we live like we're the world, because we are no longer of the world. (Confused yet?)

God is making us His people, a holy people, set apart to do His work. We are here, but our focus is not.

Lot lived in the city with evil people. We do, too.

When the angels went to destroy the city, because of its wickedness, Abraham pleaded, "If you can find ten righteous people, will you spare the city?" The Lord said He would.

When the angels reached the city, Lot 'protected' the angels from men who wanted to molest them. Lot offered his own daughters instead (Genesis 19:1-29). They said no. Lot could not even influence the city for a 'lesser' evil.

But the city had influenced Lot. He had no ministry. He had no influence, even with his own family. When angels warn him to flee the city before its destruction, he couldn't influence the men who would marry his daughters to leave, even to save their lives.

The city's sin was enough for God to destroy it.

God spared Lot and his family, dragging them from the city before the fire fell. Was it because of Lot's righteousness? Or Abraham's intercession?

Lot's wife looked back and turned to salt.

Lot's daughters caused him to get drunk and had incest with him.

Was Lot in the world but not of the world? No, the evil got into Lot.

His earlier choices affected his future consequences. Lot was selfish and chose the best land. He chose city comforts over dependence upon God. He wanted acceptance over influence.

Lot is an example of a man who focused on his best, his comforts, his acceptance. The world got into Lot. He was in the world and of it.

Are we any different? Given the choice, wouldn't you want the best? Don't you like comfort? Don't you want to be accepted?

So how do we live in the world but not be of the world?

How much of the world is in you? How would you know it?

BEING IN THE WORLD, BUT NOT OF IT: ABRAHAM'S STORY

We live in a sinful world. We are sinful people. But God calls us to "be holy, for I am holy." I Peter 1:16

How can we be in the world but not of it?

Abraham was called the friend of God. He was called to be separate from the world.

God called Abraham from his family in Haran to a land He would show him (Genesis 12:1-9). Abraham separated himself from what he knew.

How separate are you from the world? Are you living so close to the world, "snatched out of the fire" (Jude 1:22-23), that no one can tell you are a Christian?

Know the world.

When Abraham went to Egypt, he feared Pharaoh would want his wife. (Genesis 12:10-20) That's what happened. Abraham knew the world.

We should not be of the world, but we should not be ignorant of what the world does. Jesus warned his disciples, "I send you out as sheep in the midst of wolves; so be shrewd as serpents and innocent as doves." Matthew 10:16 We are with them, but should not act like them.

Do not fear the world.

Abraham knew what the world would do, but he feared the world. He responded like the world. He lied. When in Egypt, he told his wife, "Say that you are my sister so that it may go well with me." Genesis 12:11-13

Abraham feared the world and it cost him.

He did not want to be of the world, but he wanted to be safe in the world.

Sometimes I fear what the world will do to my boys. Can they live in such an evil world?

The world will not treat them nicely. In fact, Jesus said, "They will hate (them)." John 15:18

Fear hinders trust. Tell your fears to God. Does God take away the evil? No, but He helps teach you to trust Him, in spite of the evil. "For whatever is born of God overcomes the world; and this is the victory that has overcome the world—our faith." I John 5:4

I don't have to fear the world. I need to trust Him more.

Don't hold to the world's things.

Abraham knew the world, but he didn't depend upon it.

When Abraham and Lot's shepherds disagreed over land, Abraham trusted God's promise. Instead of fighting (the world's way of solving the problem), Abraham said, "Let there be no strife between you and me ... separate from me: if to the left, then I will go to the right..." (Genesis 13:7-9)

He did not cling to what God gave him. He offered it as a gift to his nephew. He didn't choose what he wanted, he accepted what God gave. He saw the green pastures that Lot took. His own appeared barren, rocky and mountainous. How could he fatten his flocks on that? He did not trust the world's things. He put his trust in God.

When Abraham chose God's way, God said, "Lift up your eyes...for all the land which you see, I will give it to you and to your descendants forever. I will make your descendants as the dust of the earth..." Genesis 13:14-18

Abraham trusted.

Sharing God's gifts, he was blessed.

God gives us gifts of the world: possessions, talents, money. Do we cling to or fight for them? Do they consume us? Or are they gifts from God to be used for Him?

Be a stranger.

"Abraham...obeyed...lived as an alien in the land of promise, as in a foreign land...for he was looking for the city which has foundations whose architect and builder is God." Hebrews 11:8-10

This is not all of life. We are strangers, not yet home.

Being in this world, but not of it required Abraham to be separated unto God. He knew what he left, yet trusted God with where he was going. He focused not on what he missed, but on Him Who gave it all. He couldn't wait until he lived with Him.

Abraham, not perfect, yet friend with God. Living in the world but not of it, yet struggling while he did. We have an example.

BEING IN THE WORLD, BUT NOT OF IT: HOW DO YOU DO IT?

How do you apply the principle, "Be in the world, but not of it"? We live in an evil world. Evil is all around us. What do we do about it?

A man gave this wise advice, "When the world starts affecting you, then you need to get out of the world."

My husband worked with a doctor who did transcendental meditation. It affected the way he ran his practice. I felt the evil when I entered the office.

Should my husband not work there because of the evil? Or should he show the true peace only God could give? He stayed. His ministry grew as others saw the contrast.

God gives us armor to stand against evil. We can resist evil.

Gird your loins with truth.

Wear the breastplate of righteousness.

Shod your feet with the gospel of peace.

Hold the shield of faith to extinguish the flaming arrows of the evil one.

Take the helmet of salvation and the sword of the Spirit, which is the Word of God.

Pray always in the Spirit. (Ephesians 6:11-20).

It is a battle that we fight until our life is done.

Evil does not stagnate; it grows. When the evil at the job was changing not the practice, but my husband, we knew it was time to leave. He found another job. Was the job change convenient? No. Was it a 'better job'? No. But we fight or flee evil.

"Therefore let him who thinks he stands take heed that he does not fall. No temptation has overtaken you but such as is common to man, and God is faithful...will provide the way of escape also, so that you will be able to endure it." (I Corinthians 10:12-13).

No one is strong enough to stand against evil alone. We will fall. But God gives us a way to flee so we don't have to fall. It's not just temptation, but 'evil.'

Joseph ran from Potiphar's wife when she seduced him daily. The consequence of running seemed hard (he was falsely accused and imprisoned), but evil did not control him. He escaped. He stood firm, trusting God. (See Genesis 39:6-21).

"Submit therefore to God. Resist the devil and he will flee from you. Draw near to God and He will draw near to you." (James 4:7-8).

We can live in the world but not be of it. There is victory. There's an escape.

Don't be weary in well doing.

IT'S THE LITTLE THINGS THAT MATTER

Ever notice it's not the big things that wear you down, but the little things that are there all the time?

Like the matchbox car you step on in the dark.

Or the mosquito bite you shouldn't scratch.

Or the sand stuck in your shoe.

No one enjoys learning the punctuation rules. But notice the meaning change when a simple comma is omitted: "Let's eat, (pause) Grandma." Or "Let's eat Grandma."

In writing, it's the little words that add or take away meaning. 'Stand up' is redundant, just 'stand' will do; don't say 'sit down,' just 'sit' will suffice; not 'he nodded his head,' just 'he nodded.' (What else would he nod?)

Those little, extra, added words hinder the meaning. Readers lose interest. The message is diluted.

By removing redundancy, words gain strength. Conciseness gives authority. The meaning is clear.

John knew this well. "The Word became flesh, and dwelt among us." John 1:14. He also knew the power of the right little words when he said, "For God so loved the world that He gave his only begotten Son, that whoever believes in him shall not perish, but have eternal life." John 3:16

So often, we discount the little things in our life as unimportant: that unkind word, that sloppy job, that ungrateful attitude. We are not perfect, but we can give our best, every time, with everything. "Whether, then, you eat or drink or whatever you do, do all to the glory of God." I Corinthians 10:31

Give those little things—that meal, that next phone call, that word—the best you can.

Will stepping on that matchbox car in the dark change your life?

Probably not, but those little words you say afterward may give glory or shame to your God. It's the little things God sees.

WRONG BELIEFS, WRONG POLICY: WRONG OUTCOME

We live in a desert. It rains less than 10.9 inches per year. The fire department fines residents for not clearing brush around our homes or weed-wacking our properties.

We have congresswomen who mandate smog control, requiring $1700 parts to be added to cars that do nothing for the car's function, but allow someone to feel like they have cleaned the air. (And create a million dollar tax base for our leaders.)

For the last ten years, logging has been banned in our national parks. Dead trees are not cleared away.

Government instituted a 'no use' policy for the understory of the forest in our national parks. Sheep and cattle used to graze the parks, minimizing the dry brush under the trees. Now through the 'no-use' policy the understory has grown.

Enter a drought since 2011.

And one lightning storm, not accompanied by rain.

One tree hit by lightning started a spark on July 31st.

We now have a fire.

Over 3,000 firemen per shift worked to put it out. Tents, trucks, and equipment covered the Squaw Valley rodeo grounds, library grounds, and the entire block of the Squaw Valley 'proper'. At their shift change at 7 AM all their big equipment and pickups headed up the hill to the park.

Water dropped on the flames only evaporated before reaching the fire.

News reported the fire licked up acres (140,000) of national forest, while these men risked their lives, daily, to fight it.

Firemen battled for a month and a half with no success.

Containment was 0%. Evacuation of areas close to the park were enforced. Roads were closed. Children from an elementary school were bused to schools in the valley. Smoke was so thick the stars couldn't be seen one hour away from the fire. The sun rose red every morning, trying to shine past the thick overcast brown cloud cover. Planes landing in Fresno, two hours away, had to land through a thick, brown smoke.

Until September 13th.

Ten bulldozers sat at the top of Hwy 180, waiting.

Waiting for what?

Because of policy in our parks that does not allow removal of underbrush, cutting of dead trees, and bulldozing, the firemen had to wait until the fire reached the outside of the park before they could effectively fight it.

We expected them to fight a fire, without allowing them access to the tools they need to do their job.

Once the fire reached the park border, those waiting bull-dozers made fire breaks to prevent fire jumping. By the end of the week it was 68% contained, after 142,000 acres had been burned. Just one week after allowing the firemen their tools to do their job.

Of course the unseasonal rain that dropped on Tuesday and the cooling temperatures (from the high 90-100 to the 70's) helped.

We have elevated creation above man. The firemen saved a certain tree from fire, but they weren't allowed to remove trees to prevent a community from being evacuated. We preserve the land, not for the future, but from human use.

Instead of worshipping the Creator, we worship the created. And we forget the people He came to save. Our hearts have been darkened. We don't know truth.

In the midst of all this smoke, I spent thousands of dollars trying to pass smog tests (imposed by the government) for two of our vehicles. Ironic? My vehicles really add that much pollution to the air?

Who's polluting my air? Who's the one paying for their wrong policy?

Look at government policy and evaluate what we are worshipping and who they are controlling. And remember our Creator.

TOO MUCH TO HANDLE

When things in your life seem too much to handle, when the 24 hours in a day are not enough, remember the mayonnaise jar and the two cups of coffee.

A professor stood before his philosophy class, waiting to begin his lecture. When the class began, he wordlessly filled a very large, empty mayonnaise jar with golf balls. He asked his students, "Is the jar full?" They agreed it was.

The professor then poured a box of pebbles into the jar. He shook the jar lightly. The pebbles rolled between the golf balls. He asked again, "Is the jar full?" The students again said it was full.

The professor next poured sand into the jar. The sand filled all the remaining crevices. He asked, "Is the jar full?" The students responded with a unanimous, "Yes."

The professor then brought two cups of coffee from under the table and poured them both into the jar, filling the empty space between the grains of sand. The students laughed.

The professor explained, "The jar represents your life. The golf balls are the important things—God, family, friends, your passion, health—and if everything else was lost and only they remained, your life would still be full.

The pebbles are the other things that matter like your job, house, or car.

The sand is everything else—the small stuff. If you put the sand into the jar first, there is no room for the pebbles or the golf balls. The same is true with life. If you spend all your time and energy on the small stuff, you will never have room for the important things.

Pay attention to the things that make you happy. Play with your children. Take time for medical checkups. Take your spouse to dinner. There will always be time to clean the house and fix the garbage disposal. Take care of the golf balls first—the things that really matter. Set your priorities. The rest is just sand.

One student raised her hand. "What does the coffee represent?"

The professor smiled. "Glad you asked. No matter how full your life may seem, there's always room for a cup of coffee with a friend."

Source:

Gaitan, Marcey. "The Mayonnaise Jar and Two Cups of Coffee." Hot Chalk Lesson Plans Page: Lesson Plans by Teachers for Teachers. n.d. http://lessonplanspage.com/imayonnaisejarand2cupsofcoffee-htm/ (accessed August 2016).

DO YOU STAND BY GOD?

The Israelites worshipped God in a tent while they journeyed to the Promised Land. They didn't build a temple until King Solomon. David asked God in Psalm 15, "Who may abide in Your tent?"

See if you would pass the test and stand by God.

1. Do you say, "I love God; He is first," but struggle on Sundays to go to church? Do you doubt things will work out for good if you obey Him?

Verse 2: "He who walks with integrity, and works righteousness, and speaks truth in his heart."

2. Do you have a friend you can share everything with, but then she shares those things with someone else? Are you that friend?

Verse 3: "He does not slander with his tongue, nor does evil to his neighbor, nor takes up a reproach against his friend; in whose eyes a reprobate is despised, but who honors those who fear the Lord."

3. Do you share the problems of others?

Verse 3: "... does not slander with his tongue ... nor takes up a reproach against his friend."

4. Do you promise to do something but then change your mind when something better comes up? Does your word mean something?

Verse 4: "He swears to his own hurt and does not change."

5. Do you keep track of grievances? Or favors? Or obligations? You may never think to bribe, or would you? Do you share with others, for them to share with you?

Verse 5: "He does not put out his money at interest, nor does he

take a bribe against the innocent."
If you passed the test...
Verse 5: "He who does these things will never be shaken."

Is it any wonder God stands in His tent, alone?

WHAT DO YOU TREAS-URE?

R ecently plans to evacuate our area because of uncontrolled fires made me ask, "If I had fifteen minutes to throw together what was important to me, what would I choose?"

Nothing seems important that I can't live without it, until...

My son helps in a ministry to clean sites after fires.

"What do the victims miss the most?" I asked him.

"Pictures, identity cards, journals and sentimental things, like a grandmother's wedding ring."

What important papers must I bring: birth certificates, marriage license, SS number cards. All in the safe, protected, ready. (By the way, safes aren't fire-resistant. Many open a safe after a fire and see nothing but ashes inside.)

How could I bring all the family photo albums for 25 years?

My husband's Bible is a treasure—he's had it since college. The cover is off, pages are loose, but he knows where to find things.

My address book contains all the addresses for our once a year newsletter. Some addresses have been crossed out multiple times as they have moved over the years; others remain the same after 25 years.

Would I sacrifice my photo books for the boys' treasures? We only have so much room. Or would it be, grab what you can hold and get in the car?

What would my sons value?

What about all our animals? How could we move them? 3 dogs, 2 cats, hamsters (one about to have babies), ducks, chickens, milking cow with 2 calves, 2 horses, plus cows at other pastures farther up the hill...am I remembering all of them?

I hold on to so much stuff. Stuff that doesn't matter. Stuff that's replaceable.

What will last?

"Now if any man builds on the foundation with gold, silver, precious stones, wood, hay, straw, each man's work will become evident; for the day will show it because it is to be revealed with fire, and the fire itself will test the quality of each man's work. If any man's work which he has built on it remains, he will receive a reward. If any man's work is burned up, he will suffer loss; but he himself will be saved, yet so as through fire." I Corinthians 2:12-15

When all is gone, what is important?

Jesus helps my focus. He said, "Where your treasure is, your heart will be also." Matthew 6:19-21

I find my perspective. If everything was gone, but all were safe, I would have peace.

WHAT IS THAT TO YOU?

John 21:18-22

I notice green yards and think of water waste.
The Lord Reminds me, "I'm teaching you, not them, to trust."
I nod. It's my lesson.

Pride slips in quickly. I ration water, I have no yard, I can trust God, but I see they do not.

I see the disciples doing the same in John 21:18-22.

Jesus tells Peter, "When you were younger, you used to...walk wherever you wished; but when you grow old ... someone else will bring you where you do not wish to go."

Peter saw the disciple whom Jesus loved following them, "Lord, what about this man?"

Jesus said to him, "If I want him to remain until I come, what is that to you? You follow me."

The Lord's words ring in my heart when I want to be someone's conscience and tell them what to do. "What is that to you? You follow me."

I sigh, because again my focus is not on the Lord. I'm not focusing on the water anymore, but I see what others should be doing (according to my lesson.) My focus is again off the Lord and He tells me again, "Follow Me." So like our children who say, "You did this for so-and-so. Why can't I do that?"

You see beyond the immediate and say, "It doesn't matter what he does, you just obey."

We know the lesson for them; we quickly forget how it applies to us.

Our Father reminds me, sometimes not so gently, "What is that to you?"

Again, I sigh. I'm so easily distracted, so easily filled with pride, so easily not following the Lord.

The words ring in my ears, "Follow Me."

WHAT HAS CHANGED?

I recently was looking through old photo albums. What dreams, predictions, and promises! I laughed at what I thought was so important back then. I knew it all (well, most of it.) How simple of me! What I thought was so important...yet don't even give a thought to now...Have things changed?

Don't I still dwell on things so temporary? What should I make for dinner? Why do I save this?

My mom recently moved to live with my sister. My sister has been sharing pictures for us sisters to claim mom's things. Things she no longer can use or want.

Memories come...piano books where I struggled to find the right keys. A tray reminding me not only of my mom but of my grandma. But as I put my claim on some, hoping I'm not taking what others will want, do I cling to memories or will I make more memories with what I take?

I've been going through my things again. What's essential? What clutter! A memory. A forgotten use. Tucked away in some corner for tomorrow. I've forgotten the use, but I still feel the memory of how useful it once was.

One of my sisters died, how many years ago? I keep her memory by her things. Is her memory any less without the thing? How do I part with sentiment? With a part of that lingers over another time...

Isn't that why God told His people, "Make a memorial?" Stack stones here, so you remember.

Aren't we a forgetful people? We get busy with today. We only remember the promises when we look back to where we once were. We forget what God has done when we think about tomorrow. Has He changed?

I have changed. My simple pleasures have added a bit of fluff. I like comfort, security, knowing expectations. I still can't just pick up and leave, but nor must I prepare for everything—I don't need diapers and toys anymore. But I will take water.

My needs have changed. I want beauty not just ugly function. I long for quiet not just filler noise. Maybe the rose-colored glasses of youth have just scratched enough to show me that perfect isn't here. Beauty awaits me in heaven.

What has changed? Me. I'd like to think my changes are because I know God better...but I doubt it. I change sometimes more than the wind with the weather. Those changes are unsettling.

What gives me security? God still keeps His promises.

I find My God is still there. Christ is all I need.

THE BIBLE WITH A HEART

What does a book do for you?
When I read, I enter a different world, where problems are solved at the end of the book.

Where an average, every-day person met unsurmountable obstacles, yet still came out okay.

Where mistakes, no matter how bad can be fixed.

Where hope still reigns.

Where good can be found.

Where strength brings victory.

That's why I like the Bible.

Good wins.

Hope is found.

Strength comes.

Answers are there.

When I go to the Bible, I see people, just like me, who have problems, made stupid mistakes, yet still held onto God with the hope—and promise of a good ending.

The Bible made me want to be an author, because in its pages, I find answers to life's problems. But more than that, I met the Author of the Bible Who gives purpose for what I share.

When you read the Bible, do you see the people as real people? Or do you rush for the principle to help you through the day?

Rushing for the principle won't allow you to find the gem. The principle lies beneath the feelings of the people.

David cried to his Lord for mercy. Without feeling David's sin, his desire for forgiveness, his longing for his heart to be right—can you see the Lord's mercy?

Mary, the mother of Jesus, pondered all these things in her heart. Can you experience the wonderment of the water turned to wine at the Wedding of Cana? Do you sense the pain of a son grown up, destined to die for her?

Lot lost his family to the world. He left his future sons-in-law behind in a city destined to be destroyed because they did not heed his warnings. He left his wife, not even knowing that she turned to salt, because he was told not to look back? Feeling remorse from choices that did not meet God's standards, he knew it when he made them, but he wanted what the world offered. It cost too much.

The Bible speaks of heart issues: forgiveness, confession, trust. It exposes hidden pain to bring healing. It shows your need to make you complete. It gives you dreams, and makes them come true.

How does it do this?

When you read the Bible,

You meet the God Who made your need so He could complete it.

You feel the God Who felt your pain, so He could bring healing.

You find wishes, you didn't even know you had, and rest in the God Who makes them possible.

You find the heart of the Bible by meeting the Author.

You find He is sufficient.

You can depend upon Him.

You can rest in Him.

You can know Him.

He is enough.

Do you read the Bible? Do you feel the Bible with your heart? Can you hear its Author calling you to know Him?

The Bible is a story about real people, with hurts, needs, dreams. But it's also about the God Who made and loves those people and wants them to know Him.

That's why I write to help you meet the people of the Bible, and the Author Who makes it all possible.

Read it with your heart.

Read it to know the Author.

DEAR MASTER OF FAITH

I've always admired
The men and women
In the Bible
Who had faith.
The giants
Of our past,
Those who gave
Us our heritage (Hebrews 11).
Abel,
Who just did right.
Enoch
Who was just taken.
Rahab
Who did what she could.
The women
Who received back their dead.
All were commended
For their faith.
None received
What had been promised
(Hebrews 11:39)
Why...
So that together
With us
They would be made perfect.
(Hebrews 11:40)

Dear Master of Faith,
It is so easy
To get caught up
In the description
Of what they were
"Men of faith.'
And forget
That their faith

Was not seen,
Nor called such
Until after they did something.
I want to be
    A woman of faith,
    A lady of prayer,
    A mother with love.
But too often
    After thinking that,
    I forget
    That all those required acts—
    Responses,
    Prayers,
    Loving.
Your acts require
    Going to the root of issues,
    Responding as You would.
    Loving beyond skin deep.
    (James 2:8-13)
    Praying
      Without show
        By meeting others' needs.
    (James 2:14-17)
    Loving
      With freedom
        By triumphing over judgment
    (James 2:13)

Dear Master of Faith,
The religion
    That You accept
      Does not go back
        To what I think (doctrine)
      But what I do—
        'look after orphans, widows...'
      Keep me from being polluted
        By the world. (James 1:27)
That goes back
      Not to what I want to be,
      But what I do for You.
Yet doing is not enough,
Fore in 'doing faith'
    We come to love You more.
There is the key
    To igniting our faith
      Into actions.

That brings
  Unity,
  Completeness,
  Perfectness (James 1:2-4)
    To my life.
You, the Master of Faith,
  Has chosen
    The poor of the world,
      To be rich in faith,
    To inherit Your kingdom
That You promised to those
    Who love You. (James 2:5)

Dear Master of Faith,
May I not strive
  To have more faith,
  To desire to pray,
  To respond in love.
May I, instead, strive to love You—
  The Master of Faith,
  The object of prayer,
  The author of love,
Who will help me
  To act
    In faith,
    With prayer,
    By love.

DEAR MASTER OF FREE-DOM

I awaited the decision.
I knew
  It was just a matter
  Of time
  Before my punishment came.
I was guilty.
I deserved to die.
I laughed

At the memory.
I killed a man
  In cold blood,
  In a predetermined act.
I hated the man.
  He deserved to die.

I rested my head
  Against the stone wall.
Now, it was just a matter of time.
To society,
  I was a murderer,
  A misfit,
  A thing to be hanged.
No one wanted mercy.
All wanted death.
Even my wife
  Didn't want to see me.

My cell door was opening.
Two guards bound my hands.
  And led me out of the prison.

I looked back

For one last look.
I guess this was it.
What cruel death
    Would they give me?
My thoughts were brought back
    When I heard the guards talking.

"What do you think
    Of this Jesus?"
"Some say
    He's the Jews' Messiah.
Some say
    He's a maniac.
I don't know
    Who He really is.
But I was there
    When the Jews brought Him
        Before Pilate.
They accused Him
    Of all manner
    Of wrong.
I could tell
    They were lying.
It was a pay-off.
I watched
    Jesus's face.
This Man took it,
    Almost as if He expected it.
But He didn't say a word.
He wasn't afraid
    Nor weak.
It was strange.
    I could read hurt
        In His eyes.
Not for Himself,
    But for His accusers.
I can't figure Him out."
The other guard responded,
"They say
    Pilate's going to offer
        A trade,
        Barabbas or Jesus
For the releasing
    Of the prisoner
        For the feast."
He laughed.

"Course,
Jesus will be freed,
He hasn't done anything."
They continued
In silence.

The prisoner knew
His fate.
The Roman's worst means
Of death,
Crucifixion.

The prisoner was led
Before Pilate
In front of the townsmen.
Another Man stood
On the other side of Pilate.
He was a strong man,
But His face spoke of pain,
Exhaustion,
Yet gentleness.
Pilate spoke to the mob
With a loud voice.
"This man,"
As he pointed to me,
"Committed murder."
He described my crime.
I tried to appear tough,
To give that sense
Of calmness
That the other Man displayed.

Maybe He could
Because He knew
He'd be set free.
Maybe that's why
He had such tranquility about Him.
My mind was brought back
As Pilate turned
To the other Man.
"This Man, is Your King,
I find no wrong."
Pilate asked,
"Will you
That I release unto you
The King of the Jews?"

I closed my eyes.
I caught sight
    Of my wife in the crowd.
I didn't want to see
    Her response
        At my death sentence.
The mob began to chant,
"Release Barabbas!
Release Barabbas!"

I was free!
I could have shouted.

I was led
    Back through the maze
        By the same two guards.
When we approached the street,
One untied my hands.
The other gave me a push
    And said,
"Remember,
    That Man is dying for you.
You did the wrong.
He didn't."
    I landed on the ground.
I brushed myself off
    and went
        To where the mob gathered.
They were dispersing.

"Wait a minute,
    What was the verdict?"
"What are you worried about?
You're a free man,
    Barabbas."

I approached
    A group of men leaving the scene.
"What's to be done
        "With this Jesus?"
I demanded.

"Barabbas,
    You're a free man
But Jesus,
    He's to be crucified."
I gasped.
They're going

To crucify
  An innocent Man
And let me go free?

The guard's words kept
  Coming back,
"You did the wrong,
  He didn't."
He was dying
  For me.
Today, I should be happy,
  I'm free!
Instead,
  I hate myself.
  I hate life.
I followed the crowd
  To the road
    Jesus would travel
  From the palace
  To the hill.
I pushed my way to a place
  Near the front.
I needed
  To see Him
    One more time.
I waited
  What seemed to be hours.
Finally,
  I saw a figure
    In the distance,
Struggling
To carry the cross.

As the figure drew closer,
I couldn't believe my eyes.
Was it the same Man
  That stood beside Pilate?
His beard was ripped
  From His Face,
A crown of spikes
  Caused blood
    To flow in His eyes.
His Face was swollen
  Beyond recognition.
His arms,
  Though strong,
  Struggled

To readjust the cross
  On His Back.
As He did so,
  He glanced up.
His eyes caught mine.

I feared to let my eyes linger,
Yet His compelled me.
In them,
  I read the look of love,
    Of forgiveness,
    Of hope.
He didn't hold bitterness.
As I had done
  To the other man
  I had murdered.
He didn't offer hate,
  As I had done.
Nor did He display fear,
  As I had.
This Man,
  This Jesus,
    Gave me forgiveness.
Not spoken,
But through His Eyes.
Those eyes
  Which spoke of love.
I was free!
I was free
  From my sin,
  My guilt,
  My blame.
I was never
  To be condemned
  Of its wrong.

I watched
  As He passed me.
I saw His Back.
I knew now
  Why He struggled
  With each move,
  With each step.
The blistered poles
  Of that cross dug
  Into raw meat
  And blood

Of that Man's back.

He's a stronger Man
Than I've ever seen.
Strong outside, yes,
But stronger inside.

I searched
For Jesus's disciples.
I needed
To know more,
About this Man.
I found.
I learned
Bits and pieces.
Of how He touched
This woman
And she was made whole.
Of how He spoke
And demons fled.
Of how He taught
How to live.

In my searching
I caught sight
Of a crowd.
I approached
With curiosity.
A man was teaching,
Not about the Law,
But of Jesus.
He had risen from the dead.
It seemed far fetched,
But possible,
This Man was Someone special.
I would search the world
To know more of this Man
Who paid the cost
To set me free.

DEAR MASTER OF HONOR

Dear Master of Honor
You left Your throne
  Over the universe
    To come to Your lowly planet earth.
You laid aside
  Your kingly garb
    To dress like a carpenter.
You left
  Your proximity with Your Father
  To resort to guarded communion.

Dear Master of Honor,
You lived on earth
  As easily as on Your throne.
You wore carpenter's apparel
  As easily as Your Kings'.
You spoke of Your Father
  As if You'd never been away.

Dear Master of Honor,
You did so
  Without complaint,
  Without regrets,
  Without a sense of shame.
Why?
  You did it for us.
  You did it for Him.

Dear Master of Honor,
You took
  The abuse,
  The rebuke,
  The treachery from people

Your Hands created.
You bore
   The load of the cross,
   The suffering,
   The criminal's death
   From Your chosen.
You died
   Being stripped
    Of Your clothes,
   Being branded
   A liar,
   A criminal,
   A fraud.

Dear Master of Honor,
You did so
   Without complaint,
   Without regret,
   Without shame.
Why?
You did it for us.
You did it for Him.

Dear Master of Honor,
Now,
You ask me
   Not to be "ashamed of Your
   gospel." (Romans 1:16)
   Not just by what I say,
   But by how I live.
Doing everything
   So that Your eyes
    Looking on
   Would not be ashamed,
   Would be pleased,
   Would receive honor.
"For therein is the righteousness
   Of God revealed
    From faith to faith."
    (Romans 1:17)

ABOUT THE AUTHOR

Growing up with five sisters, Sonya Contreras asked God many questions, even when she did not like His answers. Graduating from Cedarville University and Institute for Creation Research with a Master's Degree in Science Education did not stop her questions. Marrying her best friend and homeschooling their eight sons, she found that dreams do come true, in spite of unanswered questions. Trusting God, Who knows all answers, she shares questions that matter at www.sonyacontreras.com.

www.ingramcontent.com/pod-product-compliance
Lightning Source LLC
Chambersburg PA
CBHW061751020426
42331CB00006B/1430